Acclaim for *Daring*

"Judy takes us on an emotional journey of hope and healing as she welcomes us into her story. *Daring to Dance Again* is an engaging immersion into pain, loss, and sorrow that demonstrates how God will always bring us signs of hope. This book is engaging and inspiring. I laughed and cried, nodded, and smiled as Judy shared the intimacies of her life. This is a personal and inspiring read that will transform your understanding of life."

Rev. Doug Walter, Senior Pastor,
Ashland United Methodist Church

"In her book *Daring to Dance Again* my friend Judy Sabbert does a beautiful job of illustrating many of the lessons learned in living a purpose-filled life. She has had an exceptional life with tremendous successes and great tragedies, and she has learned to find meaning and guidance to help her through the tough times. She illustrates pearls of wisdom to help the reader have hope and find their own light in the darkness. There is a dawn coming if we are willing to open our hearts and search for it."

Jonathan Amspacher, MD,
board-certified plastic surgeon

"I was completely captivated by *Daring to Dance Again*. The writing is superb! This is a love story but far beyond. If you are open to connection and are looking to heal from life's twists and turns, this book will touch you. Be prepared to tear up, know loss, love, and laughter. It is a great collection of wisdom from poets, authors, and other artists. Truly an inspired work."

Tamra Paolillo, LCSW, Family Therapist

"Life is filled with circumstances that can challenge us when we least expect it. Judy's extraordinary life and career positively impacted many. In *Daring to Dance Again*, she shares some of her deepest challenges AND the hope, healing and happiness we can find through the "pearls of wisdom" in this book. Her words provide a map that all of us can use to navigate the trials of life and to live a life that is a blessing to others."

Andrew McCrea, syndicated television and radio host

"Judy Sabbert invites us to witness the journey of her remarkable story, as she walks us through the shadows of some of life's most painful experiences—divorce, cancer, death. She rises relentlessly, courageously, never considering for a moment that giving up was an option. Judy teaches us about the 'medicine' of trust, openness, joy, love, celebration, connection, gratitude, and hope. She demonstrates what fearlessness, fierceness and calm can look like in the face of life's greatest storms."

Eileen Grace Zorn, executive coach, focusing on potentiation of gifts and alignment with soul

Daring to Dance Again

Pearls of Wisdom
for a Soul-Filled Life

Keep Hope Alive

Judith K. Sabbert

MISSION POINT PRESS

Mission Point Press
2554 Chandler Road
Traverse City, Michigan 49696
Tel.: 231-421-9513
E-mail: doug@missionpointpress.com
www.MissionPointPress.com

Printed in the United States of America.
Edited by Gary Marx

Softcover: ISBN: 978-1-954786-90-5
Hardcover: ISBN: 978-1-954786-89-9

Library of Congress Control Number: 2022905666

For my husband DJ and our family

Contents

Introduction
by Jordan Mica

WHEN MY MOM STARTED talking about writing a memoir, all I saw was genuine hope, light and happiness in her eyes. She undoubtedly wanted to impact other people's lives through her personal stories and experiences. This would not be the first time she influenced lives in a positive manner, though. That's kind of her thing.

My mom has since retired, but as president of the foundation in St. Joseph, Missouri, she wanted to influence communities and bring about positive change. Not just in the local community where we grew up as a family but worldwide. Her goals were lofty and the repetitive word I remember her associating her work to was, "innovative." My mom's creative mindset was contagious and helped the nonprofit flourish. People from around the United States and other parts of the world wanted to know more about the programs she and her team were developing to bring about transformation in communities. The highlighted programs were to help kids build leadership and civic engagement skills and be available to schools and kids from all backgrounds.

As you can imagine, in the community my mom is viewed as a strong, independent woman who is intelligent and brings a whole lot of poise and grace. I promise you she did not tell me to write this. She broke down barriers that hadn't been broken before. Her work was such a significant piece of her life, and it truly impacted other lives. It made us kids feel proud to say she's our mother.

As important as her work was, she always made her kids her main priority. We have gone through our fair share as a family, but my mom is always guiding us through it all. For example, this woman would come home from a long day of work and still manage to whip up meals like her famous chicken fajitas, filet mignon, and homemade mashed potatoes for my brothers and me. I tell you all these things because I want to help paint the authentic picture of Judith Kay Sabbert before you read her wonderful stories.

One thing that I am grateful for is my mom and I being on the same page when it comes to spirituality. This really blossomed more after I graduated from college. Before college, we attended church regularly as a family and would talk about God and our beliefs freely. When we started to experience loss together as a family, our faith grew even stronger. She writes about some of these stories of loss in the book, and every time I read them, it makes my eyes well up with sad, yet happy tears (which is a trait I get from my mom). We are both open to signs from beyond us, and they just keep pouring in. Nowadays, some of my favorite times are when my mom, DJ, and I share stories of recent life experiences we've encountered that were no doubt a sign from above.

My mom's stories will bring you endless hope and encouragement. They also provide proof there is something wonderful out there we don't quite understand or aren't meant to understand on Earth. Keep your eyes, heart and mind open—you never know what signs you will start seeing from God and your angels after reading *Daring to Dance Again.*

Preface

JANUARY 31 HAS BECOME known in my life as a time of new beginnings. It was the day I married my first husband in 1981 and the day, twenty years later, that my children and I moved out of our house with a divorce pending. It is also the day I retired from a thirty-year career at Heartland Foundation. Today just happens to be January 31, 2018, my last day as a career woman. A time to commit my intention to sharing these stories while creating new ones.

Writing these stories is not easy for me. They are personal and sometimes intimate, and I am an extremely private person. When I told one friend I planned to write this book, he asked, "Why would you want to do that? To share your most personal and vulnerable moments in your life? I don't understand why you would do that."

"To give inspiration and hope to others going through challenging times in life," I replied.

For the last five to six years, family members and close friends have encouraged me, even urged me, to write this book, to share the many life experiences that have inspired and awed me—and others.

Here's my truth.

There are no coincidences. And God and what I've come to know as my guardian angels have led me on this extraordinary journey called life.

I've spent the last few days of my career as president of Heartland Foundation not in the office but vacationing and hiking the Red Rocks in Sedona with DJ, my husband and soul twin. We quietly reflected not on retirement, but on re-"fire"-ment. What better place to do so than in Sedona, Arizona—a sacred place, a place of healing, a place to re-fire.

I dropped off DJ at the airport, and now I am sitting alone in the hotel, waiting for Jordan, my twenty-nine-year-old daughter. I will spend another few days in Sedona with her, and she will help me celebrate the start of this new life of adventure. As I wait for her, the stories are starting to take shape in my mind, and pearls of wisdom are revealing themselves in the lessons I've learned in life.

Yet a part of me questions whether it is too late to commit to writing about my life's experiences. This morning, before his departure, DJ and I met with our friend Deena Lee. Deena is a spiritual, medical intuitive and healer.

It seemed providential that DJ and I met with her this morning on this first official day of retirement—January 31. As the three of us chatted, Deena knew I had intentions to write this book. She has a way of jumping from one topic to another, but at some point, you realize all of those topics and her stories are connected.

During our session this morning, I revealed to her that after announcing my retirement, people would tell me how much I had inspired them. I hadn't talked to some of those people in more than a decade or two. I was moved to hear from so many of them.

Deena then asked, "What does the word 'inspire' mean to you?" I said it's a word that when you hear it you just know what it is or means. She asked me to tell her more. I suggested it's when someone or something touches your life deeply, and it gives you hope. She said, "It actually means 'in spirit.'"

I love that meaning. All the inspirational stories or special moments in my life have a spiritual connection. I asked again if it was the right timing to tackle this book, and she said, "As long as it's not about EGO—Edging God Out—but it is meant to inspire others in spirit."

So, with pen and paper in hand, I start down the path of sharing my truth—those inspirational moments that have led me and, quite frankly, changed my life forever.

Judith K. Sabbert, January 31, 2018

Chapter 1

Shattered Glass

THE PICTURE OF A perfect family, a framed photograph ... how easily it slips from your fingers.

In the spring of 2000, Larry and I attended a national conference in Orlando, Florida. As we had planned, I came home to St. Joseph, Missouri, after several days while he stayed another five days to take part in a leadership program.

We both had satisfying careers for most of the nineteen years we had been married. He was an executive vice president for a local bank, and I served as the chief operating officer for a regional nonprofit foundation. Because of our high-profile positions in the community, we participated in nearly every civic and charitable event. We had two sons and one daughter, and we were very involved in their school, sporting, and other activities. At home we played games, ate dinner at set times, and rode bicycles together. We were the perfect family. That was our photograph.

The children and I had been looking forward to having their dad back, but when he returned from Florida, he seemed distant. Something was wrong. Larry had been unusually quiet for a few months, but I gave it no mind. As the next few weeks passed, however, he withdrew from normal activities, and it was hard to ignore. On weekends and evenings after work, he would run quick, out-of-the-ordinary errands or trips to get a cup of coffee from McDonald's. Always by himself. Whenever I asked him if everything was okay, he would simply shrug and say it was nothing.

Then, one day Larry announced he would be leaving for a couple of days. He was to meet with the executive bank leadership team in St. Louis to talk about a project idea he had. This was unusual. An alarm bell went off in my head. I suggested I take time off from work to go with him. We could have a little alone time away, I said. Just the two of us. But he insisted I not go.

We were both in our forties, often called the "midlife crisis" years, and, over the past year, I had to face the realization that I might not be as attractive to him as I once was. But we had the near perfect family life.

Or so I thought.

While he was away, I happened to pick up the monthly AT&T bill and noticed one unknown out-of-state number had been called repeatedly, sometimes two or three calls a day. I did not recognize the number, but I recognized instantly what was going on. I couldn't move. I couldn't catch my breath. Tears fell. My husband was living a double life.

When he returned, I could hardly speak to him, and he was more distant than ever. I finally confronted him about the telephone bill. He said it was nothing, just a friend who needed someone to talk to about a rough time she was going through in her life. I didn't buy a word of it. Later I found out they were in the same national leadership program in Orlando.

I suggested we see a family counselor. His response was less than enthusiastic, but he agreed to go. During the joint session with the therapist, I heard my husband of nearly twenty years blurt out, "I'm too far gone."

My heart sank. All I could think was, "What just happened here?"

And I knew without a doubt my marriage was over.

Months earlier, we had made reservations for our family to go to Big Cedar Lodge at Table Rock Lake for summer vacation. Larry wanted to cancel the trip. Thinking the time apart would be a good thing, I decided to make the trip with just me and the kids. It was the first time to experience what life would be like without him.

In the next few weeks before the vacation, our relationship changed dramatically. I wanted distance from him. I was angry and hurt. I kept replaying things in my head, and I didn't know what hurt the most. Was it the sudden discovery of a suspicious phone number on a monthly bill or the slow-motion revelation about his frequent trips and unexplained absences from home? Or was it his desire to travel alone, the scent of another woman's perfume, lipstick on his collar?

Today, twenty years after the divorce, none of that matters. What does matter is that this was the time when my life started to take on new meaning. This is when I started down the road that led to a deep inner peace. This is when my story really begins.

The kids and I went by ourselves and settled in at Big Cedar Lodge. Larry and I still hadn't talked to the kids about our troubles, but they could sense something was wrong. I had been losing weight, I was sad, and their father wasn't on vacation with us. Ryan, our fifteen-year-old, seemed particularly aware something big was up.

As we were unpacking in our cabin that first day at the resort, Ryan suddenly suggested we all go to church on Sunday. So, we did. We found a small United Methodist church in the Ozark Mountains and joined others in the congregation. Quite honestly, I was just going through the motions, but I found church to be comforting.

The next day we were heading to a lake attraction and pulled up to the toll booth. The older man sitting in the booth looked inside the car, noticed my three children, and nodded at me. As I rolled down my window, he politely motioned me to step out of the car and come to the booth. I did what he asked, not knowing what he wanted. He lowered his head to the window opening and discreetly said, "You're going to be okay!"

Stunned by his words, I said, "My marriage is in trouble." My hands, now trembling, were on the window ledge, and he gently took my hand in his and said he and his wife would keep our family in their prayers. And he would ask his church to surround us with prayers at the next Wednesday night church service. He asked for my first name and where we lived. A sense of peace and calm fell over me in that quiet and unexpected exchange. It felt like a God moment.

A few weeks later, Larry left for a week to attend the next session of the national leadership program in Colorado Springs. And, yes, I knew she would be there. On his way back to St. Joe, he called to say he was on the road. I asked, "How are things?"

"Well, probably not very good," he said. Reading between the lines, I knew he had made his decision. He chose her. When he got home, the family gathered in our kitchen, and he told the kids we were separating. He moved out of the house that night.

My husband and I had been married for twenty years. Getting through the divorce was bitter, brutal, and extremely painful. Your whole world and what you were once comfortable with in life are suddenly shattered and turned upside down. Routines change. Friendships change. Family traditions change. Life changes.

I lost twenty-five pounds in a short period of time,

and I didn't have that weight to lose. Eating was the last thing on my mind. Months passed and then, one day—it was like an awakening—I saw the hollow look in my children's eyes. Two of them went through traumatic weight changes. Having noticed my rapid weight loss weeks earlier, Ryan confided in me that before he heard about the separation, he thought I had cancer.

Facing all of us was the uncertainty in wondering how life would change. Admittingly, it felt as though I was scaling Mount Everest without climbing tools. The kids, too, were going through their own grief and loss.

Hayden and Jordan, who were eight and ten years old, slept in my room every night for the first year. Each night before bedtime, I would read short stories to them. Then, before turning out the lights, we said the Prayer of Jabez found in 1 Chronicles 4:10. The story goes that in the midst of his brokenness, Jabez called out to God asking Him to release abundant blessings and protection by saying:

> *"Oh, that You would bless me, and enlarge my territory, that Your hand would be with me, and that You would keep me from evil and harm, that I may not cause pain."*

Those simple words provided much comfort, strength, and inspiration for each of us.

It's been said that you have friends in life, and then you have friends for life. Karen and I became best friends for life when we met through a young women's community leadership organization in St. Joseph some fifteen or so years earlier when my son Ryan and Karen's daughter Kylie were just babies. We quickly bonded as new mothers, community leaders, and a common value system related to faith, family, work, and community. Karen was a licensed clinical social worker and primarily focused on middle school and high school girls. Her compassion, caring, and sometimes tough-mindedness brought special insights to life-altering situations.

In those first few months of the separation and the divorce, Karen called nearly every day. It was consoling to have her honest, and sometimes forceful, advice. One night she stopped by with a gift, a copy of the book *I Hope You Dance* by songwriters Tia Sillers and Mark D. Sanders. The book came with a copy of the CD by Lee Ann Womack, who had a hit with their song of the same name. The song lyrics, especially the second verse, were spot on:

I hope you never fear those mountains in the distance
   Never settle for the path of least resistance
   Living might mean taking chances, but they are worth taking
   Lovin' might be a mistake, but it's worth making
   Don't let some hell-bent heart leave you bitter
   When you come close to selling out, reconsider

*Give the heavens above more than just a passing
glance*
And when you get the choice to sit it out or dance...
I hope you dance.

Those words mattered.

It was important I have someone to talk to who wasn't close to the situation, so in those months leading up to and through divorce proceedings, I met with a family therapist. The therapy sessions were essential to keep me moving forward one step at a time as I searched for inner guidance.

Those sessions helped me stay focused on my children. I did not malign or speak negatively of their father because I knew it was important for the kids to establish new relationships with him. I knew our family would change, and the kids and I had to deal with those changes together.

Beyond those therapy sessions, though, my friends were my rock.

Karen told me three other couples we sometimes socialized with were also going through divorce. It's hard to see friends splitting up. Karen acknowledged all of these divorces had caused her and her husband, Mark, to ask themselves whether they were doing everything they should to nurture their own marriage. So, they re-examined their relationship. It turned out to be a therapeutic and enriching exercise for them.

One day, while volunteering for a benefit for the local art gallery, I was approached by a matronly woman who wanted to speak with me. The news of my impending divorce was still a bit fresh to most people, and this person had obviously heard about it. And she had an opinion. She told me her Friday night supper club was meeting that evening, but she was offering no invitation. She was delivering a not-so-subtle message. She went on to inform me there was a single woman in her age group who had been attending their social gatherings and how uncomfortable it was to have an unattached woman there among them. I was taken aback. But I knew right then that these social settings would never be the same for me.

My friend Carol told me about some of the challenges she faced as a new widow and mother some years earlier. We both experienced some of the same changes in our new lives as single women. We were no longer accepted in the social circle of couples' activities and events. Yet, as a career woman closely connected to the community, I was still expected to attend fundraising galas and other civic engagements. It was a trying experience for me in the beginning. Before entering the room at any of these gatherings, I would first have to sneak a peek at the crowd and then take a deep breath before walking through the doors on my own.

Sensing my discomfort, Karen and Mark offered to pick me up and escort me to these affairs. They were my guardian angels in those moments. In that phase of my life, some of the anxiety of feeling unwelcome was in my own head; some of my discomfort was due to very real sources. I will say, the majority of people

I encountered during those times truly did open their arms and embrace me.

I am a deeply spiritual person, more spiritual than religious. You will not find me in church every Sunday, but I believe in Jesus, I practice the Christian faith, and rely on my guardian angels for inner guidance and gentle nudging. I also firmly believe in eternal life. As my pastor, Adam Hamilton, says, "I not only believe it. I'm counting on it."

Through this time of transition, I leaned heavily on reading daily devotionals and the Bible.

Another cherished friend, Sheri, often shared scripture with me. One verse she repeated over and over to me was, "The battle is the Lord's." (1 Samuel 17:47).

Sheri also gave me several books by T.D. Jakes to read. One of his motivational books, *The Lady, Her Lover, and Her Lord,* acknowledges that: "No matter what sorrow life has brought before you, don't stop until you see morning, because morning does come .... Overcome obstacles with confidence. Survive traumas with triumph .... Find solace through sorrow and know comfort in the midst of crises, because the morning does come."

After a period of grieving, I realized and understood I had to find the strength to heal and let go. I accepted that my life—and my children's lives—would be quite different. One friend advised, "The normal traditional family you once had will never exist again." He was right. I knew we had to find our "new" normal. It was time to stop going through the motions of life with intense, almost scarring sadness and an overwhelming feeling of fatigue from little sleep night after night. Somehow you do find the inner strength to take one step at a time. Morning does come.

Filing for divorce in early September of 2000, the transitioning time of separation and deep reflection taught me I was capable and strong enough to be a single mom. As someone once said, "You never know how strong you are until being strong is your only choice."

Creating normalcy for our now family of four was so important. We maintained the routines we had established long before the troubles began. We'd play board games after school and work—Scrabble, Scattergories, or Bobble—and we'd ride bikes in the neighborhood. We would have candle-lit, sit-down, home-cooked meals as often as possible, and sometimes my kids' friends joined us for family mealtimes. Their favorite meals were chicken fajitas for dinner and pancakes for breakfast. Oh, and Gold-N-Glaze Donuts on Saturday mornings.

The first year, and for many years after, we would take a short vacation over the holiday break. We explored some big cities—Chicago, San Francisco, Charleston, and New York—and we took a Royal Caribbean Cruise and snow skied in Colorado and Utah. Keeping the family together was my priority and preserving old or making new family rituals let my kids know, "I've got this."

During that time of healing, I discovered that you create your own world, and it does take an immeasurable amount of no-holds-barred courage to squarely face the immense obstacles and difficulties in front of you. It requires setting your intentions to find the raw power and passion to move forward. With a commitment to hard work and God's grace, I knew it was possible.

Early in the divorce process, my friend Rhonda gave me what became one of my favorite bibles, *NIV Women's Devotional Bible 2*. It contains a collection of daily readings along with the scriptures from the Old and New Testaments.

One of the devotionals was called "Shattered Glass" by Joni Eareckson Tada. I read it over and over. Joni has been an inspiration to me and so many others. As a seventeen-year-old, this young woman's first major battle in life was caused by a diving accident that severed her spinal cord. She suffered paralysis of her hands and legs. Now an artist and author, her words deeply touched my soul:

My art studio is a mess of half-chewed pastel pencils, old tubes of paint, and piles of illustrations overflowing my file drawers. Recently while cleaning up, I discovered some broken glass on the counter by the window. I also discovered that when sunlight struck the shattered glass, brilliant [and] colorful rays scattered everywhere.

Shattered glass is full of a thousand different angles, each one picking up a ray of light and shooting it off in a thousand directions. That doesn't happen with plain glass such as a jar. The glass must be broken into many pieces.

What's true of shattered glass is true of a broken life. Shattered dreams. A heart full of fissures. Hopes that are splintered. A life in pieces that appears to be ruined. But given time and prayer, such a person's life can shine more brightly than if the brokenness had never happened.

In those days, unquestionably, I experienced deep sadness and pain. Over time, I came to the realization that I needed to totally re-script my life's journey.

My life coach and mentor, Lee Kaiser, helped me put things in perspective. We met in 1994 through the national healthy communities movement. He was one of the conference speakers and a leading expert, and I was taken by his outlook on life. Over time, we became friends. He taught me so much. One insight he shared was this: "Deal with difficult people with love and grace. When a person cuts you off and hurts you, give them a blessing. Reverse the energy. When you give a blessing like that, it might just change their life. More importantly, it will certainly change yours."

I found that the problem you're facing will dominate your life until you're willing to forgive! Set your intention. With God's grace, you can do so. It doesn't necessarily mean you resolve and rebuild the broken relationship; it does mean you're able to let go and move on with your life. For me, I discovered it was time to forgive him, purposely seek what was waiting for me, and heal what was then a shattered life.

I believe God places guardian angels in our lives. Some are spiritual. Others are earth angels like the kind stranger in the toll booth, my close-knit circle of devoted friends and family, inspirational authors like Joni Eareckson Tada and T.D. Jakes, and Lee. Mostly, I give thanks to God for His divine guidance and the blessings of His angels in our lives to protect and help us rebuild our shattered lives.

A Pearl of Wisdom:

Find Inner Peace and Guidance to Re-script Your Life

Joseph Campbell said, "We must be willing to get rid of the life we've planned, so as to have the life that is waiting for us."

The life I'd planned was no longer possible. The impending divorce compelled me to redesign what was then a broken life. No matter what hardships or heartaches you may go through, I discovered there are always new opportunities ready to unfold. These new openings create a chance to both learn and unlearn how you re-script your life from the present to the future with its infinite possibilities.

Moving forward takes patient persistence in order to heal and learn the lessons awaiting you. Ask God for strength and inner guidance. Dare to believe better days are ahead, while asking yourself: What desired change do you want for your life? What is your intention? What do you aspire to accomplish in this lifetime? How you answer those questions will shape how you live your life! Your existence may take a surprisingly new direction.

With boldness and courage, you can rebuild your life. It requires transforming those self-limiting thoughts and attitudes that hold you back. Instead, live a life of discovery, love, joy, faith, and wisdom. Find the strength to be the architect of your life in moving forward. *Be intentional!*

And remember: When you have the chance to sit it out or dance, I hope you *Dare to Dance Again*!

Chapter 2

Maddie and the
Great Escape

DIVORCE IS CHALLENGING, BRINGS up raw emotions, and impacts loved ones around you. Those days when I needed some reassurance, I received words of encouragement from family and friends who reached out through phone calls, thoughtful notes, and heartfelt cards. These acts of kindness came at times when I struggled most.

After about a three-month separation, I filed for divorce in early September of 2000. A court date was scheduled by the judge for proceedings to be held the following April. The practice was to wait a period of at least six months, and give those seeking divorce ample time to reconsider their decision. The wait seemed like an eternity. I was ready to move on with my life and begin the healing process.

In the interim, my soon-to-be-ex and I agreed to put the house on the market in October. My dad was a realtor at the time, so he and my mother would drive the kids and me to different neighborhoods around town and show us potential properties for sale. Looking at homes gave us a sense of hope in a dark time in our lives. We eventually found a spec house in Carriage Oaks, a relatively new subdivision my kids and I really liked.

A contingent contract was signed with the seller to hold the property while we waited for a legitimate offer to be made on our existing family home in Oak Hills. Once that happened, we could finalize a deal on the new house for a fresh start for the kids and me. Fortunately, the house in Oak Hills sold before the end of the year, and we prepared to make the move to our new home about thirty days later—on January 31.

Our family was moving from a stately, colonial-style home to a more compact one that was half the square footage. But the open concept, split-level house with four bedrooms and a large, spacious family room seemed perfect for our family. This love for our new smaller home was validated by many of my kids' friends, who lived in houses you might find in *Better Homes and Gardens.*

Ryan was in high school and active in team sports, primarily golf and basketball. Unless he had an evening game, he would stay after school to practice

with his team. Because I worked, Jordan and Hayden
(sixth- and fourth-grade students) came home after
school. Clara, a twenty-something college student at
the local university, picked them up from Eugene Field
Elementary after school and watched them at our new
house until I came home. Oh, and yes, we had one
other family member, Maddie, a lovable and sometimes hyperactive chocolate Labrador retriever.

Because the house had never been lived in and we
took possession of the property in the winter, there was
no grass or landscaping in the designated yard space.
The nearly one-acre lot was in a field that was once a
pasture. The ground was dirt. Not one blade of grass
anywhere. Just hard dirt, plain and simple—unless it
rained or snowed. Then it became a muddy mess, or it
remained frozen. Grass seed was slated to be planted
in the spring.

Prior to moving from our house in Oak Hills,
Maddie normally stayed in the fenced-in backyard or
in a large, roomy outdoor kennel with a dog house to
shelter her from adverse weather when we were gone.
Now with the grassless yard and no fencing at our new
home, we had to make other accommodations for her
while we were away. It was clear the kennel would not
work outside in the frozen wasteland that was our lawn.
We wanted to provide Maddie a more suitable set-up.

Friends Reed and Brenda heard about our dilemma
and loaned us an indoor dog kennel, which was placed
in the climate-controlled garage. If we were gone,
Maddie could stay there until one of us returned home.

Needless to say, Maddie didn't care much for this new arrangement—at all.

As we were settling into our new place, my parents came over for dinner to spend time with the kids and me the Tuesday before Valentine's Day. That evening they brought us a large heart-shaped box of Russell Stover dark chocolate-covered raspberries. By this time, we had been in our new home for less than two weeks.

Every morning, Hayden would take Maddie on a brief walk before school. Along with the padded doggie bed, Hayden then made sure Maddie's kennel had a soft blanket for snuggling and warmth, a few toys to play with, a large bowl of drinking water, and one with dog food. Once Maddie was nestled into her new day-time quarters, the kids and I left for school and work.

My kids would have dinner with their dad after he got off work on Wednesday nights. I would either catch up on things around the house, stay at the office to work later, or meet a close friend for a glass of wine or dinner. On this particular Wednesday night, I was running errands with my friend Chris when my cell phone rang. It was Clara. She expressed how horrified she was at the scene she discovered when entering our home.

Maddie—like the Great Houdini—somehow mysteriously and not so magically managed to escape from her wire-caged kennel. She knocked over a six-foot step ladder butted up against some shelving, which hit the interior door leading from the garage into the family room. Upon impact, the door flew wide open for

Maddie. Seizing the opportunity, she made a mad dash into the house. Her Great Escape!

In her exploration of the house, Maddie found the nearly full Valentine's Day box of dark chocolates that was left on the kitchen island the night before. And, you guessed it, she had herself a feast, devouring all the delectable chocolates and leaving not a single piece.

Clara went on to explain it was quite possible Maddie also ate some rat poison, which was hidden under the television armoire in my bedroom on the second floor. A few of the toxic pellets were found scattered around on the newly laid carpet. After ingesting the chocolates and likely poison, our precious pet became sick, regurgitating everything she had swallowed, leaving a trail of diarrhea and vomit around the dining room table, the family room, and my bedroom upstairs. It was an unsightly scene.

Dogs who eat an overabundance of dark chocolate normally die, and with the rat poison ... well, it didn't look so good for Maddie.

Clara went on to explain that, before giving me the dreadful news, she called my mom, who rushed over to help the sitter clean up the mess. The two of them found Dial dishwashing detergent underneath the sink and promptly squirted the soapy liquid directly onto the soiled carpet. Not only did the soap remove the dark chocolate-raspberry diarrhea and upchuck, it also took the color out of the beige-flecked carpet, noticeably and shockingly leaving pure white, roundish spots, which were now unmistakably clean.

My friend Chris dropped me off at the house. As I opened the front door, I was also horrified. A brand-new house with wall-to-wall carpeting that had been laid only a few weeks earlier ... ruined. And quite possibly, Maddie was not long for this world. Losing our sweet pup would have been devastating to our family.

Ryan was now home from basketball practice, so the two of us loaded Maddie—all sixty pounds of her— into the back seat of his car and headed to the vet's office. Because Dr. Wes' office was closing in a matter of minutes, I called to alert the staff that we were on our way, and explained the dire emergency we faced. After examining her, Dr. Wes recommended Maddie stay overnight for observation.

It had been a hectic and crazy day, and, after the kids left to have dinner with their dad, I opened a bottle of Malbec and poured myself a glass. Before I sat down, I remembered I hadn't picked up the mail. I sorted through the envelopes on the way back up the driveway and spotted a card from my Aunt Martha in Florida.

Aunt Martha, my mom's twin sister, sent a card to me every week with a personal note expressing her caring and loving support during this difficult time in my life. She did so faithfully, and each week I would look forward to her next "thinking of you" Hallmark card. Her encouragement was just like clockwork— steadfast and unfaltering.

This card was different. Instead of one designed by Hallmark, Aunt Martha had created her own com- puter-generated card. The front featured a cartoonish dog, sitting in a chair with an overhead light brightly shining on her guilty face. Inside it read: "I'm sorry things are so poopy for you right now."

I sat down on the newly ruined carpet in the middle of the family room and laughed hysterically. Tears rolled down my cheeks. How could my beloved aunt have foreseen the day's crazy antics? One thing was for sure: My aunt's attempt to bring laughter and encouragement in her own creative way became a day brightener of the best kind.

Maddie survived the dark chocolate, and she survived the rat poison. Dr. Wes said the rat poison might have counteracted the chocolate, acting as an antidote by helping her eliminate everything she'd ingested that day. You might even say this near death experience was Maddie's second Great Escape of the day. This one from doggie heaven.

A Pearl of Wisdom:
Encourage Others

Raw emotions would well up inside me during my divorce. Not knowing what the future held for me and my kids, there were many days I just felt numb. In my confusion of what was happening, comical moments like the one with Maddie would lift my spirits. Mostly, day brighteners occurred when my friends and family unexpectedly reached out during particularly fragile and chaotic days. On that cold, wintry Wednesday in February, that's just what my aunt did. She expressed her deep love and concern not just that day, but throughout my ordeal.

Although my Aunt Martha passed away some years ago, her encouragement, compassion, and caring are still felt today. Reach out to people in their time of need and when things seem to be okay. You never know what a person may be going through, and your presence and reassurance may boost someone's life.

I once read a brief devotional passage called *Gravity at Work,* written by Sharon Mahoe. It was very fitting: "Encouragement. Doesn't sound like much, but it's everything. Send some encouragement today. You'll be a part of someone's memories for a long, long time."

Chapter 3

Angels Come in Different Forms

I ONCE HEARD THESE words, "We do not know the weight of love until it's released." Grasping the meaning of that phrase took some time. However, after losing both of my parents within a few months, I began to take in the significance of those words. It happened in 2012 when my parents departed from this world. My mother, Bertha Sabbert, passed away on March 9, and my dad, Marvin, passed away six months and one day later on September 10.

My parents spent the last five years of their lives in assisted living facilities. My brothers and I made the difficult decision to move them from their home when their health began to fail and their ability to fully care for themselves was greatly diminished. Mom had been diagnosed with dementia, and Dad fought Alzheimer's.

Both are debilitating disorders. Their doctor carefully explained the difference between the two to me and my brother Bernie. Dementia, as described by the Alzheimer's Association, is "a chronic or persistent disorder of the mental processes caused by brain disease or injury and marked by memory disorder, personality changes, and impaired learning." Symptoms can include stroke-like indicators such as muscle weakness or paralysis on one side. My mother exhibited all the symptoms including complete paralysis in her left arm. My father often repeated his stories, which were tied to special memories he treasured from decades ago.

One thing was for certain—our family felt the unspoken love our parents held for their children and grandchildren. In spite of faltering, fragile minds and everything they faced, Mom and Dad knew their children and grandchildren to the very end of their lives.

From as early as childhood, I clearly remember my father as a quiet and gentle man. This never changed. Dad loved living on the farm as a kid and for most of his adult years, but his favorite recurring story during his Alzheimer's years was talking about the time he flew his Cessna aircraft—or was it his Mooney?—to New York City.

He enjoyed flying for a good part of his life, soloing when he was only sixteen years old. It was his favorite avocation. Many Sunday afternoons, my dad and I would disappear for an hour or so to take a flight over the vast rural countryside of northeast Kansas and northwest Missouri. Although he flew thousands of flights, and a few of those were cross-country, to my knowledge he never piloted his plane to the Big Apple. Without a doubt, it was a long-held dream he cherished.

Near the end of each nursing home visit, Dad would nod off to sleep, quietly snoring in his favorite brown leather recliner. As I prepared to leave, I would reach over and touch his arm to gently wake him. Each time I would say, "Dad, before I go, can I see your big beautiful blue eyes?" He would wake up, always with a glint in his sparkling blue eyes as well as flash his warm, gentle smile and tell me he loved me.

Mom was oftentimes distant and withdrawn, although she was always polite in those moments. I remember from early on how vivacious she had been. Stunningly beautiful, Mom always took care of herself until the wrath of dementia took hold of her mind. She was a small-town girl from Hiawatha, Kansas, the Maple Tree City. Dad was the love of her life.

The pair of them were soul mates, spending over sixty-five years together as husband and wife. My mother once shared with me that someone once referred to them as a matched set—just like salt and pepper shakers. They were. Unique personalities with different gifts and talents and yet very much a dynamic duo. They complemented each other in the best way possible. A matched set indeed.

Another story Bertha would take pride in, and often remind Marvin and "us kids" about, was the candy bar story. Evidently, my dad had an interest in a girl named Betty who was a high school classmate from Hiawatha. In getting to know this young woman, he held out an Almond Joy and a Hershey's candy bar, asking her which one she preferred. Betty pondered for a moment, then greedily grabbed the two bars from his hands and said, "I like both." Needless to say, her hasty and selfish decision ended my dad's pursuit of this classmate.

Once he noticed a tall and lanky girl named Bertha with shoulder-length, dark brown hair, and he decided to apply the same "girlfriend" test as he did with Betty. He held out two candy bars—again an Almond Joy and Hershey's bar—and asked if she'd like one. Bertha quizzically looked at Marvin for a brief moment and replied, "You choose the one you want." Needless to say, he chose Bertha.

Two years after high school graduation, Marvin and Bertha were married and settled on a farm a mile outside of White Cloud, Kansas, a town with a population of nearly 300 people at that time. This small-town young woman, now a farmer's wife, was always a sophisticated lady. She dressed fashionably, wore bright ruby red lipstick, and was a beautiful person inside and out. With a spicy personality, she was not afraid to speak her mind. Both were loving and generous—finding ways to serve and give back—and quietly helped individuals in their times of need.

Now, decades later and with Mom's battle against dementia, she lost her zest for life. She rarely cared about her personal appearance and hardly ever initiated conversation. Such a change from the proud woman we all knew so well.

My three brothers and I were so concerned for her well-being, and the knowledge that we were losing her to this dreadful disease was more than we could bear. Her doctor recommended we take her to a rural hospital just thirty minutes away in Cameron, Missouri. Dr. Rippe ordered a full-blown behavioral and mental health assessment for a two week-long observation. He believed medical experts from the Geriatric Center for Behavioral and Mental Health Unit might give us some answers. We did so with my mother's stern objection, and her silent treatment was felt as soon as she received the distressing news.

My mother was clearly angry with her children for making this difficult, yet necessary decision. Her irritation continued as she refused to speak to Bernie and me all the way to Cameron. Upon arriving and checking Mom into the residential medical facility, we spoke with the center's staff about her frail condition. As Bernie and I were ready to head back to St. Joseph, they asked that the family wait several days before visiting her. It was absolutely devastating for us to leave our despondent mother behind.

As soon as we had the doctor's permission, my brothers Rick and Bernie and I went to see her. We couldn't believe the difference in her mood and now upbeat state. She actually laughed, joked, and told stories. Her care plan included a psychological assessment, medical testing, an adjustment in her medications, and a vitamin K injection. We were cautiously optimistic that "Bertha was back."

Jordan, then twenty-three years old, was especially close to Mom. Many times, in the past when Jordan came to visit her grandmother, Mom would be lethargic and communicate very little. I encouraged Jordan to give her grandmother a phone call, noting the immense change we had seen in her. This time when Jordan called, Mom answered the phone with, "Well, hi, Love Bug." She appeared to be her old self— talkative and engaged.

As they chatted on the phone, Jordan broke down and cried as she told her grandmother how worried she was about her. Mom said, "Oh, sweet Jordan, please don't cry. There's no need to cry. It's like I've been living in a cloud, but I've always been here. I just couldn't respond to you, but I'm here now." Jordan told her how much she loved her, and Mom said, "I love you, too."

Unfortunately, it wasn't long until Mom was back to her depressed, unemotive state. There were a few exceptions, however, and on those occasions one of the caretakers would call to let me know it was a good day for Bertha. I would dart out to see her, aware that the next day—or even the next couple of hours—would most likely be different. Those precious moments when she had bright spots were treasured.

Two weeks before she passed, I received another

phone call from the caretaker, Sandy. Bertha was back.
When I arrived at the care center, Sandy shared that
she had asked Mom where she was going all dressed
up. Mom joyfully told her, "I'm getting ready to go to
heaven." When I entered Mom's room, she was just
as Sandy described—all dressed up, her hair carefully
coifed, and donning her ruby red lipstick. Indeed,
Bertha was back.

Days before Bertha passed away, she had devel-
oped pneumonia, and when her condition worsened,
she was rushed by ambulance to the nearby hospital.
As soon as I received the call, I made my way to the
emergency room some two miles away. As I entered
the treatment room, I sensed her time was near. She
gasped for every single breath. I gently touched her
arm to let her know I was there. She turned her head
in the opposite direction, refusing to look at me. Later,
my chaplain friend, Sally, who was serving as the hospice director at the time, told me it's not unusual for a
loved one to turn away when they are in the process of
dying. It's a way of separating from loved ones and the
world they are leaving.

The ER attending physician stepped away from
my mother's bedside and asked to talk privately with
me about her condition. The next words out of his
mouth were, "I need your permission to intubate your
mother." I tearfully explained that she had a Do Not
Resuscitate (DNR) order filed in her medical record.
The doctor acknowledged he was aware of the DNR,

but continued to press that if the procedure wasn't started within the next ten minutes she would likely die. Dismayed by his request, guilty feelings welled up inside of me as I felt pressured to make a life-or-death decision in that moment. Even though I feared losing my mother, I hesitantly replied, "You need to honor my mother's request—*do not resuscitate*."

A short time later, Mom's breathing became a bit more normal, and she survived the medical crisis that evening.

Bernie and I spent the night with her in the assigned patient room. The next morning the hospitalist okayed her transfer by ambulance back to the nursing home where she was reunited with my father.

A few days later, the doctor placed Mom in hospice care along with Dad, who was now diagnosed with congestive heart failure. Reality set in that the end of my parents' time on this Earth was near.

Less than twenty-four hours later, I was driving out of town on US Route 36 to Cameron for a meeting with the Northwest Missouri Regional Economic Developers Association when I received a call from the nursing home. Mom was in distress, and the nurse's tone sounded grave, as if Mom's death was imminent. I turned the car around and headed straight for the assisted care facility.

My three brothers were called. At that moment, my sister-in-law Angela was taking Bernie to the ER for a medical treatment of his own; Rick left as soon as he could get on the road from St. Charles, a four-hour drive away; and Doug would arrive later that night from Kansas City.

When I entered my parents' suite, two caregivers, a hospice nurse, and a hospice social worker were tending to Mom. My father sat cozily in his recliner watching sports on TV in their small living area, completely unaware of what was going on in the next room.

I remember the moment like it happened yesterday. Mom's breathing was shallow and labored as she gazed in my direction. As she closed her eyes tightly, I walked over and sat on her bed, reached to hold her hand, and talked with her about cherished life memories we shared. Even though she was unable to communicate, the facility's owner, Connie, who was now present, assured me she was listening. I held on to the thought that Mom was taking in every word. I related more family stories and told her how she made an impactful difference for her family, friends, others, and the world. Her life mattered. I kept thinking there was so much more I wanted to say—a lifetime of precious memories; and yet, I sensed her time was passing much too quickly.

She then opened her eyes widely and looked at me intently. Now trembling, I wondered what she was thinking. She must have known her time on Earth was ending as she lay there gasping for every breath, still unable to speak. But her big brown eyes said it all. They conveyed her love—a mother's deep love. During that time, the hospice nursing staff attended to her needs: checking her vitals, giving her pain medication, and making her as comfortable as possible.

I told her our time on Earth is like the blink of an eye. I shared my belief that life is eternal, knowing in my heart and in my soul that we would again be together someday.

Toward the end, Rick arrived from St. Charles. We quietly greeted each other, then hugged tightly as we spoke softly outside my parents' suite in the hallway. As we entered the suite, Rick gently embraced Dad and talked with him for a while. With Dad still content to be watching TV in his favorite chair, he was unmindful that his wife lay dying in the next room.

My older brother Rick is a lawyer, photographer, and lay clergyman. He immediately assumed the role of pastor as he said a prayer while we gathered around Mom's bedside. We both expressed how deeply we loved her and conveyed it was okay to let go and join her parents, her twin sister Martha, and close friends Ruth and Virginia who were all joyfully waiting for her to cross over and come home.

As Mom was close to passing, I wondered how I would know that she was okay. At that moment, a vision of a brightly colored, red-breasted robin popped into my mind. For me, robins represent new life, so it was the perfect image to hold onto.

In a matter of a few short minutes, my beloved mother took her last breaths as Rick and I watched her peacefully cross over. She was no longer in pain, and I could only imagine the heavenly celebration as the angels and past loved ones embraced her soul.

Bertha's funeral was scheduled four days later on March 12, 2012. That morning, Ryan, his fiancée Kristen, Jordan, and Hayden were getting dressed to leave for the funeral at Ashland United Methodist Church. As I waited for the kids in the dining room, I glanced outside the front window and could not believe my eyes. A single robin sat perching on a limb of the pin oak tree in front of our house. Not just a robin. It was the first robin of springtime. An amazing light brightly shone behind the bird— almost like a halo. Angels do come in different forms, and I instantly knew ... Bertha was home.

Once Mom passed, we all worried about Dad and how he would handle the grief of losing his wife and soul mate, sharing more than sixty-five years of marriage together. He seemed to be very aware of her death during the funeral service. Throughout their married life, my parents were inseparable. They worked together, played together, raised four children together, and deeply adored their eleven grandchildren and one great grandchild, Evan.

Days later, Bernie and I met with a geriatric psychiatrist to seek advice on how to help Dad deal with Mom's death. He advised that the most humane thing to do is not acknowledge her death. So anytime our family visited with Dad, who now had full-blown

Alzheimer's, he normally would ask where Bertha was. All of us responded, "She's okay, Dad, and you'll see each other soon."

It seemed to pacify him until the next time we were together. Again, every visit he asked, "Where's Bertha?"

With the deterioration of Dad's mind and his short-term memory loss, he was unaware that she had died. If we told him she was no longer alive each time he asked the question, it would be just like hearing the unbearable news for the very first time. Why would we want to bring agonizing, untold grief upon him again and again? I recall only one time when Dad asked, "Judy, did your Mom die?"

I softly responded, "Yes, Dad."

He replied, "I thought so." Just two days later when I visited him, he once again inquired, "Where's Bertha?"

Dad passed away six months after Mom. Both had strong convictions about their family, their work ethic, and their faith. While Mom had the spicy personality, Dad had a calmness about him. He was a soft-spoken, gentle man who quietly influenced his family and those around him. A businessman, farmer, stockman, risk taker, entrepreneur, community contributor, husband, father, and grandfather extraordinaire!

My brothers and I knew it was only a matter of time before he would pass away. After Mom's death, the nursing home transferred Dad into the secured Alzheimer's unit. I dropped in often and feared each time he was slipping further away from us. Even though it was difficult knowing his time was short, every visit was cherished.

I felt blessed that only once in the course of his disease that Dad did not recognize me. We had been visiting an hour or so, sharing the same stories over and over again, when he needed to go to the bathroom. A nearby caregiver offered to take him. About ten minutes later when she rolled him back in his wheelchair from the bathroom to the place we had been sitting, the caregiver said, "Your daughter's still here."

He had a blank look on his face and responded, "I have a daughter? How nice!"

We had been reminiscing about life just ten minutes earlier, but now he had no idea who I was. It was heartbreaking. I stayed and shared more familiar stories with him, as he smiled and laughed. Before leaving that day, thankfully, he recalled that I was his daughter.

A few months later, Dad took a turn for the worse. Jordan was home for the weekend, so we stopped by to see him on the Sunday before he died. Lying in bed with his eyes closed tightly, his body quivered and teeth chattered as he quietly moaned.

We sat beside him, holding his hand while talking to him. Still he never opened his eyes or responded in any way. When it was time to go, we said goodbye and told him how much we loved him. Before leaving, Jordan asked her grandfather for a kiss.

Then, unexpectantly, he opened his eyes and mustered the strength to sit up in his bed. He reached out and gently kissed both of us. As we were leaving the facility, we related our story to one of the caregivers. She commented it was a "God thing" that my dad could gather the strength to kiss us goodbye. As Jordan said, "When people are in terrible, deep pain, somehow they still find a way to tell you they love you and always will."

Watching a loved one die is difficult; it can be an emotional and spiritual thing. We both knew his life's journey would soon be over, and we felt like he knew it, too—even in spite of the Alzheimer's.

A couple of days passed when one of the nurses called to let my family know Dad's condition had worsened, and we should come as soon as possible. Bernie, Doug, and I all arrived at the nursing home as soon as we could.

Dad's big blue eyes were closed tightly the whole time we were there. For a couple of hours or so, we talked to him about his life, our family, unforgettable memories, and the impact he had made for each of his four children and the world around him.

The hospice nurse checked his vitals and thought it would be okay to take a break. My brothers and the caretaker stepped out of the room. I stayed.

All at once, Dad's breathing became shallower, while his eyes remained tightly closed. I realized he was close to taking his last breath. As his breathing became more and more labored, I asked him if he would open his "big beautiful, blue eyes, just one more time for me, before you leave to be with Mom."

Remarkably, he opened his eyes wide and looked directly into mine. I shared with him my story about Mom's passing and the robin vision that came into my mind just before she died. I said, "Dad, my sign for you is not just a robin, but many robins. That's how I'll know you're okay."

As I embraced him, I heard someone enter the room. I assumed it was one of my brothers. As my father took his last breaths, I held him close and did not want to let go. My entire body trembled uncontrollably.

Holding him for some time, I knew he was home, back in the arms of his devoted wife. I finally let go and realized the person standing behind me was Sally, my dear friend and hospital chaplain director. The hospice staff had notified her that my father was in the process of dying. Sally reached over to hug and comfort me and then said a prayer for Dad.

I told Sally I couldn't stop shaking as I held him in those last moments. She said, "Judy, that's not what I observed. I saw you gently holding and lovingly rocking your dad." I think my angels must have been surrounding me, while they gently embraced and rocked me.

Jordan was aware of the request I made to her grandfather for a sign he was all right. The morning of Dad's funeral, as my kids and Ryan's now wife, Kristen, were all getting ready, I screamed with joy for the kids to come downstairs.

I had peered out the front window and was both

overjoyed and overwhelmed with what was happening outside in our front yard. My request was granted. Sensing something remarkable was going on, Jordan hurried down the stairs and walked over to see what was happening outdoors.

Speechless, we both stepped out onto the front porch. Dozens of robins—and I do mean dozens—were flying around the front yard. They were only in our yard in a neighborhood where many houses surrounded us. In fact, there were more than a hundred birds and many different species. It felt as if we were surrounded by angels. I've had encounters like this before, yet this one was beyond anything that had ever happened to me.

While driving to the church, my kids and I noticed two lovebirds sitting atop the concrete wall of the overpass. Another sign my parents had reunited.

After church services and the burial at the graveside, my brothers and their families came by our house. We reminisced a number of stories about our precious parents and the love we shared for them. Sitting on my back deck, I suddenly realized the birds had returned. Hundreds of them. Butterflies, too. My brothers were also there to witness this amazing, indescribable sight.

The next morning, I was alone. Everyone had returned to their homes the evening before. I looked out the kitchen window and noticed my feathered friends were once again congregating in my backyard. In my leopard-skin, flannel pajamas, I stepped outside and sat in the middle of the concrete basketball court to take in this beautiful, awe-inspiring, and sacred sight.

Birds soaring high up into the sky. A flock of hundreds of birds. The celestial celebration was like a gift sent from heaven.

Then, out of the blue, the birds all quietly landed in the backyard. I counted more than forty robins. Yes, robins. Dad and my angels came through for me. Not only did I see one robin, I saw many robins. Every bird I could imagine was in my backyard. Cardinals, summer tanagers, wrens, sparrows, hummingbirds, blue jays, a red-headed woodpecker, finches, meadowlarks, a whippoorwill, and species of birds I could not identify.

Taking it all in, I began to sing the hymn "His Eye Is on the Sparrow."Many years earlier, my mother requested this song be sung by the congregation at her funeral. So, we did. The inspiring hymn was also sung at my father's funeral. I had no doubt God and my angels were watching.

Losing track of time, I sat motionless in the backyard when the most mystical and spiritual sight occurred. The feathered creatures lifted off the ground and surrounding trees all at the same time, airborne directly over me and my house, and were never to be seen again. I knew in the deepest part of my soul that my guardian angels were close by. What a joyous occasion it was! The birds were jubilantly celebrating my parents' reunion, and there was no doubt in my mind.

Angels come in different forms.

A Pearl of Wisdom:
Believe in a Higher Power

Dying is a sacred journey. Sitting at my parents' bedsides as they each actively went through the process was agonizing and sorrowful, but I'll always cherish those moments. As I reflected on their lives in those last few hours, I recounted how they lived long and blessed existences. They touched so many people with their love of humankind, generosity, joys and sorrows, and the example they set for others to embrace the fullness of life.

I believe our angels are meant to guide and provide loving support during our time on this Earth. No doubt my angels did so as my parents were dying. My angels were present, and they confirmed my parents' souls were liberated. Bertha and Marvin had both blissfully entered heaven as our family witnessed indescribable celebrations of their departures. Their spirits filled every inch of the sky as the angelic birds departed. I felt the weight of their love being released to those of us left behind. To this day, my parents' love continues to envelop me and deeply touch my soul.

Our guardian angels provide grace-filled guidance, protection, and comfort to us on an unending basis. They send signs and messages that are personal and recognizable just for you. It is consoling, uplifting, and reassuring to know that through His angels, God sheds His love and mercy on His children.

Like Jordan shared when she discovered a sign on the day she sat at her grandfather's bedside, "Life is better when you believe (in a higher power)."

Chapter 4

Lady in Red

FOR THE FIRST TEN years after the divorce, I was focused on raising my kids and managing a highly stressful career. My family and profession were the top priorities. People often asked why I did not pursue another relationship during that time, but I felt strongly that bringing another person into our lives was not in my children's best interests. My life was full and complicated enough from balancing all aspects of being a single mom, a civic leader, and a professional career woman. Dating was simply out.

Even as the kids were becoming young adults—with one in graduate school, one in college, and one a junior in high school—the possibility of dating was nowhere on my radar ... especially when it came to seeking out a serious relationship. I had resigned myself to staying single and, quite frankly, was prepared to remain unattached the rest of my life.

It wasn't until Hayden was a senior in high school that I accepted a date with a longtime friend, Mike. He was someone I trusted, and we always enjoyed each other's company. It was safe and comfortable. Mike lived in another state up north. When he came to town to visit friends and family, we would go out for an evening meal, attend a concert, or just make dinner at my house. After a number of months of casual dating, the distance was clearly a barrier to building a deeper relationship, so we parted ways.

Dating Mike did make me realize it was time to consider finding a new partner. I'll always be grateful to him for that.

Shortly after, my kids encouraged me to pursue online dating. I looked at Match.com and instantly decided it wasn't for me. It's Just Lunch—a Kansas City dating service—seemed like a better option and much safer way to meet eligible men with similar interests. I did meet some interesting guys. However, with only a few exceptions, I had no real interest in seeing them beyond the first face-to-face meeting. These guys were nice enough, but we had very little in common. In fact, the few I did go out on an official date with also quickly turned out to be incompatible partners. Maybe dating was not such a great idea after all. And I certainly wasn't the type to date just for the sake of dating.

Later, I signed up with a matchmaking dating service out of Kansas City. After numerous strikeouts,
my matchmaker introduced me to a man named Ken
whom I started to see casually over a couple of months.
At first glance, we seemed to be fairly compatible. Both
of us had professional careers, were civic leaders, had
grown children, and enjoyed many of the same things
in life. And I must say, Ken was extremely attractive.
Still, something just seemed amiss.

Then I received a call from Ashley, my matchmaker, who wanted to introduce me to Dennis. She
said, "Judy, I have someone I'd like you to meet."

I hesitated and told her, "I'm not really interested."
Reluctant to develop a deeper relationship with Ken, it
seemed as though I was incapable of finding love again.

Ashley insisted and shared, "You don't understand!
This guy is a perfect match for you. At least meet him."

She then told me a little bit about this man, and,
with her persistent urging, I decided, "Why not? It's
only dinner."

Dennis called me a few nights later. We talked
briefly before he asked if I'd like to have dinner on
Friday night. I shared with him that I had already made
plans to go to the Lake of the Ozarks for the weekend.
I was heading to the Sabbert family cabin to spend
time with my son Ryan, his wife Kristen, my daughter
Jordan, and her boyfriend, also named Ryan. What I
didn't tell Dennis was that I also invited Ken to come
along. I thought my children could help me figure out
what to do with this guy.

As I pondered the date request from Dennis, I again recalled Ashley's plea as her words began to resonate, "You just *have* to meet him. He's perfect for you."

I will say that when Dennis first called, I liked the sound of his voice. Sensing he thought I just wasn't interested in going out, I boldly suggested to him, "What about getting together the next weekend?" Plans were then made to meet him the following Friday night at Zona Rosa, a high-end shopping district in north Kansas City. In the meantime, I had the lake weekend coming up in a few days with my kids. Oh, and Ken.

Ken was fun to be around, but the relationship seemed to be more like a brother and sisterly one. Was I too picky or just afraid to pursue a serious relationship? Just as I thought, after my kids met Ken, they were totally honest with me. Kristen summed it up best, "They're just not a match." It was the last time I saw Ken.

Now with Ken no longer in the picture, I was even more curious about this new guy. The week leading up to our first get-together, Dennis and I texted one another a few times, which was a newly acquired skill for me. Then, as I was getting ready for work, another text came through to confirm our date at the Italian restaurant Bravo! in north Kansas City. He ended his message with: "So we can find one another, I'll be wearing a lavender polo shirt and black pants. I have salt and pepper colored hair, and I'm six feet tall. How will I recognize you?"

I replied, "I'm currently a blonde, five feet, ten

inches tall with heels, and have absolutely no clue what I'm wearing tonight. Looking forward to meeting you."

After work, I ran home to get ready for my blind date. Looking through my closet, I debated on what to wear. Still having no clue, a sleeveless bright red dress with gold metal buttons popped up among the other dresses in my wardrobe. I grabbed it, hurriedly got dressed, threw on my three-inch black heels, and put on matching gold earrings and a bracelet. Oh, and just a splash of Thierry Mugler's Angel perfume. Standing in front of the floor-length mirror, I thought as I gazed at my reflection, "Here we go again, Judy."

I rushed out to the garage, jumped in my car, and headed to Kansas City. With the radio blaring and playing to seventies music, I once again wondered how this evening would play out with this new man, especially as I thought of Ashley's insistence that this guy was perfect for me.

Usually, I would call one of my closest friends to let her know I was meeting someone new and where I would be that evening. That way, if something went horribly wrong, at least the police would know where to start looking. However, this night I did not. I somehow felt deep in my soul that this guy just might be different from all the others.

I was parking the car about a block or so away from the restaurant when Dennis sent a new text. "I'm standing outside in the courtyard, listening to the band I arranged for our first date. Meet me there!"

Every week during the summer, Zona Rosa hosted

Friday Night in the Park, where bands would play in the open air. "I love this man," I said out loud. He had a sense of humor. I texted back: "Just now parking. Oh, BTW, I'll be the lady dressed in red. And ... how very thoughtful of you to arrange a band for our very first date. See you in a moment."

The park was adjacent to the outside terrace of the restaurant. The terrace was normally at full capacity, especially on Friday nights when you could dine while listening to the band. How thoughtful for him to book a table there, I thought.

I told the hostess I was meeting someone on the terrace, and, as I picked my way past dozens of tables and all of those diners, I tried to steady my nerves. My heart was beating rapidly, and my palms were warm. At the back door, I took a deep breath and stepped onto the terrace. Okay, where was he? Where was this six-foot-tall man with salt and pepper hair, a lavender polo shirt, and dark slacks?

Nowhere.

I could hear the band down in the park. I looked around the terrace again, checking more intently this time. Couples and foursomes were enjoying cocktails and dinner, talking and laughing. Others had flocked to the bar, hoping to grab a barstool. But my date was not among them. I asked one of the bartenders if he'd seen a man fitting my date's description. Nope, he said, no tall dudes with lavender polo shirts, nope. Now what?

I headed back inside with my red dress and three-inch heels, trying to act casual as I slipped between those same tables with those same diners, and the waitstaff hustled past me, delicately balancing trays of food and drink. The whole time I was glancing around trying to spot Dennis. I looked over at the indoor bar. Not there. At this point, I was beginning to think he had seen me, decided he didn't like what he saw, and made an early escape.

I went outside and looked around again. Still no luck. Then I decided to pull out my cell phone and reread his text. Then it hit me. He said he was "outside in the courtyard," in the park area, not on the terrace. Now running more than fifteen minutes late, I tried to recover and appear cool, calm, and collected as I sauntered over to the courtyard.

There he stood. An attractive, nearly sixty-year-old man, looking far younger than his years, watching the band play seventies rock 'n' roll—my favorite.

Dennis glanced my way. My heart actually fluttered and skipped a beat or two. I couldn't help but smile from ear to ear. I had found the elusive man. Before I could say anything, he flashed a huge grin and said, "Oh ... my Lady in Red!"

We went up to the bar on the veranda and ordered a glass of Sketchbook Cabernet while we waited for our table. Talking to Dennis was easy. We chatted about some of our favorite concerts and musical artists from the seventies. The Eagles, Phil Collins, Steely Dan, Fleetwood Mac, the Doobie Brothers. Dennis had been a disc jockey in his younger years and had a passion for music from that time—the sixties, seventies, and eighties. While in his last year of high school and first two years of college, he spun records for several radio stations in his hometown of Fairfield and Salem in southern Illinois and later in Evansville, Indiana. Now he worked for an international company known as Munich Re, a reinsurance company that provides insurance to insurance companies. As one of the regional vice presidents in the United States, he traveled quite a bit to meet with his clients from different states. It sounded impressive, but he didn't try to make it sound that way.

When our table was ready, Dennis ordered a bottle of Sketchbook, and we agreed to share a meal—chicken parmesan with sautéed vegetables and a house Italian chopped salad. We talked about our kids, family, careers, avocations, religion, spirituality, everything. The conversation flowed so easily. It was effortless.

After dinner, we walked around the shopping district. We strolled around for about an hour and then sat on a park bench and delved a little deeper into each other's stories. Neither of us wanted the evening to end, but it was getting late. As we said goodbye, I stood on my tiptoes, leaned in, and kissed him gently on the cheek. Then Dennis went home to Overland Park, Kansas, and I went home to St. Joseph, Missouri.

When I woke up that morning, I had no idea that by the end of the evening I would know.

A Pearl of Wisdom:
Stay Open to the Possibilities

Life can change when you least expect it. I know it did for me. More than a decade earlier, I had resigned and relegated myself to staying single for the rest of my life. Now, all of a sudden, I felt like a teenager who was giddy and head-over-heels with my first love. But I wasn't sixteen years old. I was soon to be a sixty-one-year-old woman, and I was a person, quite frankly, not expecting to fall in love. Let alone to find the love of my life.

Trust me. As I came to realize after meeting Dennis, true love can happen even in your twilight years. I will say that during the twelve years I was alone, I discovered who I was beyond the conventional life roles people saw me in: a mom, a daughter, a divorcée, a friend, a professional career woman, a civic leader, and a woman of faith. With life's struggles, heartaches, and unexpected joys, I matured into someone who was learning to re-script my life. Sometimes you just have to wait for the right timing. At this point in my life, it was not just about the timing. It was about being open to new ways of thinking and being.

Take a chance. Fully engage in life. Be aware of what is happening around you. By being wholly and abundantly present and having the courage to change or take a chance, you open yourself up to creating new opportunities for something positive to occur in your life. Something you may never have expected just might be waiting to happen. Stay open to the possibilities!

Chapter 5

Save the Last Dance

FOUR OR FIVE DAYS passed before Dennis finally called. After exchanging a few pleasantries, he asked me out for a date that weekend. I teased him, "So, what do you plan to do to top arranging a band for our very first date?" He laughed and told me he had tickets for the Michael Bublé concert at the Sprint Center. I immediately said, "Yes." But the show was Sunday night, not Saturday, and I had to back out. I was attending the Two Worlds Wisdom School in Boulder, Colorado, and it was to start Monday morning. My flight left Kansas City Sunday afternoon, so the date was off.

In the meantime, though, we continued to text each other and talk on the phone. Somewhere in that time I started to refer to him as DJ rather than Dennis. Clearly, he had become my all-time favorite disc jockey.

That Sunday I arrived at the Colorado Chautauqua, a historic landmark nestled against the backdrop of the Flatirons just outside Boulder. Founded in 1898, it is one of the few remaining Chautauquas in the United States, dedicated to lifelong learning, nature, music, and the arts. Often described as "an oasis of respite, rejuvenation, and enlightenment," the Chautauqua's park-like grounds are surrounded by quaint cottages, group residential housing, a fine dining hall, a general store, impeccably manicured landscaping with larger trees, a calming water feature, and a mission-inspired/ arts and crafts-style community center.

After checking into my cottage, I drove to the local Whole Foods and picked up groceries for the next few mornings. Back at the cottage, I settled in to read my paperback on the screened-in front porch while enjoying the gentle breeze and cool fall air on that Sunday evening. The book was *The Alchemist* from one of my favorite authors, Paulo Coelho.

Later that night, DJ sent me a text. It contained a video of himself and his son, another Ryan, listening to Michael Bublé on stage, singing "Save the Last Dance for Me."

"Who is this man?" I wondered.

We had difficulty finding time for a second date because of our busy schedules. On Labor Day weekend, he was heading to northern Florida to spend time with his brother and sister-in-law, while I was jetting off to San Diego with my kids to attend my nephew's wedding.

Even though we had only met in person once, we were in constant contact—communicating by phone and text. While in San Diego for the wedding, my kids wanted to know "What's up, Mom?" They knew I was not a texter, and they were quite curious about my sudden fascination with the phone. They wondered why I was acting so giddy and smiling from ear to ear. The kids even remarked, "Mom, you're texting just like a teenager!" Later that night, my children mocked and poked fun at me because my cell phone had gone off during the wedding reception dinner. It was DJ, of course.

My nephew Austin and his bride, Meredith, had a beautiful wedding, a joyous occasion with lots of dancing and laughter. Only one thing was missing: this new man in my life. It's odd to say. However, from the very beginning, we felt like we'd known each other forever and sensed a deep spiritual connection.

After dancing most of the night, I texted DJ to let him know, "I wish you were here and could dance with me."

He immediately replied, "Dance. Dance. Dance. Dance with your children. Dance with your family. Dance with other men. I just have one request, 'Save the Last Dance for Me!'" I knew I was falling in love with this man, which was so out of character for me. As someone who was prepared to spend the rest of her life single, I was definitely letting my guard down.

The next weekend DJ and I met at the Oppenstein
Brothers Memorial Park just off the corner of Twelfth
and Main Street in downtown Kansas City. I parked
my car on the busy street directly across from the park
and saw him sitting alone on a bench watching a small
wedding ceremony taking place. As soon as he saw me,
he stood up and walked over to hug me. We embraced
for a moment then left in his car and headed to the
Crossroads District for First Fridays. The festival-like
atmosphere featured art galleries, unique boutiques,
restaurants, and outdoor food and drink stands that
stayed open late into the evening.

After strolling through the crowded district, we
stopped and shared a meal at Manny's Mexican restaurant. The evening flew by. We went to the KC Power
and Light District to walk around the popular enter-
tainment area. A classic rock band was playing in the
outdoor courtyard. We stepped out onto the brick patio
and danced until midnight.

Later, as we sat in DJ's car, we were both surprised
to discover we had brought gifts for each other. DJ
gave me a handful of seashells he had collected from
the Jacksonville beach and a couple of books on spirituality. I gave him a triangular red rock—not knowing
the significance at the time—I found while hiking up
one of the trails in the Flatirons. Knowing his love for
seventies music and books on spirituality, I also gave
him an Eagles *Greatest Hits* album and *The Alchemist.*
We laughed that we had surprised each other with
gifts—not to mention that they were so very similar. I

couldn't help marveling at the fact that this was only our second date.

He walked me to my car in the cool of that September night, and, after a warm embrace in the middle of the street, we shared the most memorable kiss ever.

In those few weeks since meeting one another, everything seemed to magically fall into place. Our phone conversations and multiple texts back and forth just clicked. We exchanged information about nearly everything under the sun: our joys, our hurts and sorrows, our values and beliefs, times of grief and loss, our faith and spirituality, our love for lake life and travel, our careers and passions, and most certainly, our children and families. It was as if we had known each other for a very long time—a lifetime. The strong connection between us seemed unbreakable—like a soul connection of the deepest kind.

DJ invited me to a symphony performance in downtown Kansas City for our third date. For the first time, we met at his home in Overland Park, which meant I made the seventy-minute drive from St. Joseph.

He lived in Nottingham by the Green, an attractive neighborhood with large mature trees in a prime location of Johnson County. His stately two-story home had a lot of curb appeal, and the yard was immaculately groomed. The interior was as meticulously cared for as the exterior. He gave me a quick tour of the house, and we dashed off to dinner in downtown Kansas City, cruising away in his newly-purchased, black 300C Chrysler, which he jokingly called The Limo.

We had dinner at the Webster House before going to the symphony, and, as the hostess led us to our table and handed us the dinner menus, she asked, "Are you here to celebrate tonight?" "Yes, we are," DJ said, "It's our third anniversary." She flashed a broad smile and congratulated us on our big event, not knowing this was only our third date. We were still giggling about that when a waitress showed up with two flutes of sparkling Prosecco white wine, compliments of the restaurant, in honor of our big celebration.

Dinner was fabulous, and the symphony was spectacular. The evening had been perfect, and our feet barely touched the ground as we walked hand-in-hand back to The Limo. And that's when things took a turn.

After we buckled in, DJ pressed the button on the control panel to start the car. But nothing happened. He pushed the button again. Still nothing. DJ was beginning to fidget. I could tell he was becoming self-conscious, perhaps embarrassed that his new car, The Limo, was not responding.

He studied the instrument panel a few moments longer and tried it again. And again, nothing. Then, all of a sudden, it was as if a light went on in his head. He realized, somewhat embarrassed, that what he thought was the ignition button was actually the volume control for the radio. He nonchalantly slid his finger to the correct button. The engine began to purr. And we burst into laughter.

"This is what we call a 'Judy Moment,'" I said, "I've had more than my share of moments just like this." And we drove away in The Limo, smiling all the way home on our third date. Or was this our third anniversary? One thing was certain. I knew deep in my soul that night that it was worth saving my last dance for this man.

A Pearl of Wisdom:
Find Joy and Laughter

Noticing DJ's readiness to laugh at himself was heart-warming. What could have been an embarrassing and tense time on our third date became a bonding moment for us.

No matter what happens in your life, find spontaneous joy in those embarrassing, yet precious moments. When you have the courage to laugh at yourself, you gain a whole new perspective on the world and the people around you. Celebrate your life by making room for unconstrained joy and laughter.

Uncovering the rapture of laughter really does make a difference by touching one's soul. Not only will it brighten and uplift your day, it will also likely cheer up someone else's heart.

And remember: Finding humor in something as simple as not recognizing the difference between the radio's volume control and ignition buttons can spark a special connection and actually help you dial in to another person.

Chapter 6

That's the Angel

DJ AND I HAD known each other for little more than a month, but we already felt a deep connection. That connection was undeniable, uncanny, almost mystical.

After the concert at the Kauffman Center, we returned to DJ's house. I had never spent the night there, and now on our third date, I wondered if I should stay or if I should make the long drive home. My decision would be made for me.

Once we were inside, DJ opened the cabinet that contained the stereo system. He popped in a CD and hit the start button. It was the right button this time. And Michael Bublé's "Save the Last Dance for Me" poured softly from the speakers. DJ took my right hand and asked, "Will you dance with me?" He slipped his arm around my waist and drew me closer. I felt safe in his arms and experienced an overwhelming sense of joy and innocence. One thing was clear—I trusted this man. And I knew I would not be driving home this evening.

When we reached the top of the stairs, he handed me a card. It was the first card he had ever given me. As soon as I opened it, chills ran down my spine and tears welled up in my eyes. I literally had goose bumps. The front of the card featured a picture of a cardinal. How could he have known? I had yet to share my angel stories with him. At that moment, I realized this must be another sign from my angels.

The message on the front of the card was all the confirmation I needed:

When an angel appears
You know you are cared for.
Just open your mind to the form
Your angel takes.

Below the verse the card read *Happy Birthday*. And inside the message was:

You are surrounded by angels.
You always have been.
Now take some conscious risks with
The understanding that
Your Angels will catch you
If you fall.

The best part of your life
Has just begun.
In fact, this next year
Is going to be
Your Best Year yet.

I was spellbound, moved by the passionate verses, awe-struck at the reference to angels and birds. And then DJ said, almost apologetically, "I wasn't sure when your birthday is. I just liked what the card said."

He had written a personal note, too.

"Judy, a.k.a. my Lady in Red, Happy Birthday ... or am I early? I couldn't resist this card. As we get to know each other on a deeper level, I need to know the date of your birth!!!"

It was September 18, only days away. Everything in my soul felt right. I was exactly where I was meant to be.

The next weekend DJ was in St. Joseph, and I knew it was time to share my angel stories. I led him out-side to my backyard and onto the makeshift basket-ball court. There was a slight chill in the air, and the September sun was shining brightly without a cloud in the sky. We sat cross-legged on the concrete pad in the exact same spot I was sitting when the flock of birds of all types rallied and encircled me the morning after my father's funeral. Hundreds of them. I then opened my heart and shared the stories with DJ. I explained how I believed angels do indeed come in different forms. He listened intently on that autumn day as I related the celestial descriptions of those angelic moments to him.

It was January, and the first five months of our relationship passed. We were clearly attached. I had never felt this depth of the love with any other man. Certainly, I loved my first husband when we married, but this was different. This love was something rare and extraordinary.

We left for Sedona that month to spend a week together. On January 13, 2014, we hiked on one of the four trails considered to be a vortex—a place called Airport Mesa Loop, which coiled around the Sedona Airport. A vortex is believed to be a site that holds higher vibrational energy rising from the Earth. It's known to provide spiritual healing and energy balance. At Airport Mesa Loop and the other vortex areas, people express feeling more energized and motivated. This particular vortex trail is a stunning and challenging hike to complete with nearly 360-degree panoramic views of red rock formations. It is truly inspiring.

At times while hiking, we would pass through narrow winding passageways surrounded by prickly pear cacti, juniper trees, cedar shrubs, and other foliage native to the area. Many of the juniper tree trunks were gnarled and twisted from the silent and invisible vortex winds.

As we walked down the meandering path through a medley of trees, everything was perfectly still. No one else was there. It was so calm and quiet. And then it happened. Nearly forty tiny birds were encircling us.

The birds looked like finches, only with a bright, even vivid, teal-colored head.

The petite birds sang and chirped while orbiting us for several minutes. It was almost as if they were expecting our visit, and it felt like they were trying to tell us something, reaching deep into our souls. Then, just as quickly as they had appeared, they vanished. This astounding sight left us both speechless.

We walked just a few more feet before DJ stopped and took my hand in his. "Judy," he said, "I knew from the moment I met you that you are the one I want to spend my last trimester with. I knew my angels sent me a sign confirming you are the one when the birds surrounded us. It's as if they were looking straight into our eyes. I didn't plan for this to happen at this moment, but I've been nudged to ask you now. Will you marry me?"

I blurted out, "Yes! A thousand times, YES!!!"

It took me over sixty years to find this man. If I had to live my life all over again, I'd wait another sixty years if it meant we'd be together.

At that moment, I understood the significance of the triangular red rock I had found in Boulder and gave to DJ some months earlier. We were now standing on a ridge with the sun shining brightly on a small juniper tree, overlooking what appeared to connect several vortex areas. The invisible lines formed a triangle amid the red rock formations of Bell Rock, Cathedral Rock, and the place we were standing on along the Airport Mesa Loop. This poetic, romantic spot is etched in our minds forever and has become our special, sacred space. This is where we vowed to spend the rest of our lives together.

Hesitant to leave this euphoric moment on the hiking trail, we zigzagged down the narrow path and headed back to the car. We drove to the Tlaquepaque Square and stopped for lunch at The Secret Garden Café, one of our favorite dining spots in Sedona. Music was playing, yet neither one of us paid much attention to it while we were ordering. Then, suddenly, I heard the musician sing, "Just Say Yes." Having heard this piece for the first time, it took my breath away. Here are some of the words that resonated that day:

So ... tell me today and take my hand
Please take my hand
Just say yes, just say there's nothing holding you back
It's not a test, or a trick of the mind
Only love.
It's so simple and you know it is
We can't be to and fro like this
All our lives
The path is clear
What do I have to say to you
For God's sake, dear
Just say yes.

After leaving the restaurant, I discovered DJ heard the same song, which I later found out was recorded by Snow Patrol. Clearly, it was another sign and a message from our angels.

That afternoon, DJ and I traveled to historic Jerome, the mile-high town on Mingus Mountain just thirty minutes outside of Sedona. Once known as "the wickedest town in the West," Jerome was a flourishing copper mining town with a population of 15,000 in its heyday. Founded in 1876, the mine closed in 1953. It nearly shut the town down with only 100 residents living there at one point.

Although the mines are silent today, the town is now a tourist magnet and artist community. It boasts unique gift shops, bed and breakfasts, arts and crafts galleries, and a number of bars and restaurants. The antiquated, yet picturesque Southwestern town clearly hasn't changed its appearance much in nearly a century and a half.

We strolled hand-in-hand through the shops and galleries, and, when we spotted a local bikers bar called The Spirit Room, we decided to go in for a couple of cold ones. The place was crowded, and there was some great music from the seventies and eighties playing. The leather-clad locals were having a good time dancing, and we joined them. They readily welcomed us into their club, and we partied with them for an hour or so before we realized it was time to go. We had reservations for dinner at Dahl and Di Luca Ristorante Italiano in Sedona.

As we were leaving Jerome, we noticed an old school building that had been converted into an art studio and gallery called the Old Mingus Art Center. It was nearly 5:30 p.m. and almost closing time. We had time to make a quick stop. The door was open. We seemed to be alone. Dimly lit hallways went this way and that, leading to old classrooms full of art of different types. I stepped into one of the rooms, while DJ headed the opposite direction. Then I heard DJ's voice. He had found someone.

DJ was talking with Robin John Anderson, the artist and owner of the gallery. His studio was a large space, one of the old classrooms on the first floor. A toddler's gate fit snuggly inside the doorway to keep the dog corralled inside the studio, and I had to step over it to get into the room. The walls were covered with hundreds of original etchings, images of famous people and unknown ones.

Robin shared a bit of his life story, about living in this community and why he and his wife chose to move here from New York's Greenwich Village. He also explained his process for making an etching. Then he asked, "Would you like to see how it's done?" We said yes, and he said, "Pick out an image from the wall."

DJ deferred to me. There were hundreds of images. Where to start? There was Leonardo DaVinci, the original Renaissance man who has long fascinated me. And I was attracted to a number of drawings featuring Native Americans. These images particularly spoke to me because I grew up just miles from the Iowa Native American reservation.

But my eyes kept going back to one etching—an ethereal image of a woman with long, flowing hair and a Mona Lisa smile. I had no clue why I was drawn to this image, but it resonated with me. When I pointed to it, the artist smiled and proclaimed, "Awww!!! That's the Angel."

Tears began to stream down my face. The Angel? How could that be? But, of course, it was another sign for us that day. Our angels had brought us together. I could barely get the words out to explain to the artist why this touched my heart so much.

We watched Robin create the etching of the angel—now our angel—in front of us. DJ bought the piece as a wedding gift, and Robin signed the artwork, titled it *The Angel* and then acknowledged the date—January 13, 2014. The day DJ proposed.

We returned to our homes in Missouri and Kansas on Sunday, still aglow from our magical and spiritual trek to Sedona and Jerome but ready to get back to work the next morning. On my desk that morning, I found a small package wrapped with a ribbon. It was a gift from the local United Way, a thank you for my annual contribution as a Crystal Circle giver.

In it was a box of notecards with an artist's rendering of a bird—our bird. They were the same birds that encircled us on Airport Mesa Loop. A small, finch-like creature with a brightly colored, teal head. How could that be?

I called the United Way office, and the young woman I spoke with informed me that Glenda Hamilton's son,

Josh Hamilton, was the artist. Glenda was the major gifts officer for the local United Way.

Glenda called me back, and I told her about what DJ and I had experienced with the birds while hiking in Sedona on the vortex trail. She too was astonished and said she would have her son call me. She also mentioned Josh had kept his original painting of the bird.

When Josh called, I shared my story, and I asked him what the species was. He hesitated for a moment and said he had no idea. It was just an image that came into his mind. An imagined bird.

Josh sold me the original painting, and I gave the unframed, twelve-inch square canvas to DJ as a wedding gift. This extraordinary piece now hangs in the dining room of our home in Kansas City. These fine artworks are gentle reminders each day that we are watched over by our guardian angels. How very blessed we are!

A Pearl of Wisdom:

Be Open to Signs and Messages

DJ and I have experienced a number of amazing, life-changing events. Those occasions have lifted our spirits as our angels have inspired, guided, watched over, and protected us. We know for certain that these experiences are more than coincidences.

Have you ever had a sign, message, or missive placed in front of you? Whether a natural wonder, a piece of artwork, song lyrics or a musical composition that speaks to you, or a vivid dream or some other communique that has an underlying significant meaning, your guardian angels are the gentle voice of your soul. Watch and listen for them!

Too often, we get distracted in the busyness of everyday life and miss the messages and signs that are directed at us. Pay attention, or you will easily overlook the blessings and the grace-filled guidance that is there for you.

Chapter 7

A Judy Moment

WE'VE ALL FACED EMBARRASSING moments in our lives. I've certainly experienced my share of what I call "Judy Moments." In *Webster's Dictionary*, you would likely find the following definition of a Judy Moment:

(ju´ dee mo´ ment) *n.* **1.** A brief, unexpected event that is oftentimes embarrassing, **2.** A startling event produced by a reasonably bright person, **3.** A particular interval of time that emits belly laughter.

Here is one example.

For nearly fifteen years at the Cattle Baron's Ball, I have donated a live auction item for the annual fundraising benefit that supports Heartland Foundation youth programs. The in-kind contribution was a dinner for eight in my home.

This is no ordinary dinner party. I strive to make this a magical evening by being at the guests' beck and call from the minute they arrive until they depart. Sure, I enjoy the event as much as they do, but the goal is to make them feel as if they were dining at a Michelin star restaurant. The dinner menu consists of gourmet lasagna with all the trimmings—including appetizers and a variety of fine wines (of course). The grand finale—the icing on the cake, if you will—is a made-from-scratch, three-layer Italian cream cake, one of my mother's recipes.

The lasagna recipe is a secret that I hold to this day. It was from a former college boyfriend's grandmother. He has no clue that I have it—which is part of the fun. Yes, you might say I stole it, but it's been well worth it. The recipe has raised over $20,000 for the Heartland Foundation over the years. I honor the fact that it's a guarded family recipe and haven't shared it with anyone, not even my own children, who constantly beg me for it.

On the night of the January 2014 Cattle Baron's Ball, Dr. Lindy Andrews, a dear friend of mine, had the winning bid for the dinner for eight, and a date was scheduled soon after the gala.

DJ and I had known each other for five months at this point and had just been engaged to be married. This was his first time to be immersed in the Foundation's annual gala, and I was pleased he enthusiastically agreed to help me prepare the dinner and to serve as the bartender that evening.

We worked like a well-oiled machine in getting everything ready for the party. The groceries and a wintertime bouquet of flowers were purchased the day before. The house was decorated, and the dining room table was set with my best dishes, stemware, and tableware. On the morning of the big event, the ingredients for the eight-layer lasagna were assembled into a special, oversized baking pan and placed in the refrigerator, making it easy to pop in the oven around 6 p.m. right before the guests were to arrive. Early in the afternoon, the appetizers were prepared, a Caesar salad tossed, and veggies cut, seasoned, and ready to go into the oven at the right time. DJ made his famous guacamole dip as one of the appetizers; it was set aside to be savored before dinner with the multi-colored bell peppers and sea salted, blue corn chips. I don't believe I am telling any secrets when I relate that he adds the stems from the cilantro to his dip, giving it a burst of flavor.

Now 2 p.m., it was time to tackle the cake. I pulled out *A Few of My Favorite Things,* a book created by my mom, and subtitled "From the FILE of Bertha Sabbert." Mom's book is a trove of her best-loved recipes, but it is more than that. It contains keepsake photos of Mom and Dad in their journey through life, starting as infants as well as photos of her children and their families through various stages in life.

In another section, she shared her thoughts and

reflections about the uniqueness and special qualities of her eleven grandchildren. Personalized greeting cards sent to her from my children and me that she especially cherished were saved over the years and placed in the *Favorite Things* book.

Mom also shared her thoughts on how to live life successfully and with grace. This section included hints and tips from newspaper clippings of columns written by Ann Landers, Heloise, Erma Bombeck, and others.

And she loved reading the Sunday morning cartoons in the *St. Joseph News Press* and clipped those she relished most—*Hagar the Horrible*, *Hi and Lois*, *The Family Circus*, and *The Lockhorns*. I can picture it now. Mom in her robe, and Dad in his pajamas sitting around the kitchen table, chatting and laughing about the comics while drinking coffee and eating Gold-N-Glaze Donuts.

I had made Mom's Italian cream cake with cream cheese frosting many times, and my fingerprints were all over the plastic sleeves that protected the pages of Mom's *Favorite Things*. I had picked up all the baking ingredients the day before, so I started measuring out each one to make it easier and faster to prepare.

Being reasonably familiar with the recipe, I thought I knew the steps quite well and decided to take a shortcut by simply reading the ingredients list. The cake batter recipe called for:

- 2 cups sugar
- 5 eggs

- 1 stick oleo
- ½ cup Crisco
- 2 cups cake flour
- 1 cup buttermilk
- 1 cup Angel Flake coconut
- 1 teaspoon baking soda
- 1 cup chopped pecans
- 1 teaspoon vanilla

The oven temperature was preset for 325 degrees, and three round cake pans were greased and dusted with flour. With only a few hours before our guests would arrive, I added each carefully measured ingredient into the aluminum mixing bowl one by one, using a hand-held Sunbeam electric mixer to blend them together. Done. Everything was coming together smoothly. Almost too smoothly.

As I was ready to pour the mixed ingredients into the greased and floured cake pans, I noticed the batter did not have the right consistency. It lacked the fluffiness you would expect. I went back to the recipe, this time reading the step-by-step instructions thoroughly. I was aghast to discover that an earlier step called for the five eggs to be separated and to add only the beaten egg yolks. The very last step in the process was to beat and then fold the egg whites into the batter.

Ugh! I had to start all over. I threw the first cake batter down the kitchen drain and pulled out all the ingredients again, precisely measuring each one while grabbing another five of "Eggland's Best" from the carton in the fridge.

Now even more rushed with guests expected to arrive in less than two and a half hours, I hastily remade the batter, only to realize I had once again forgotten to separate the eggs. What was I thinking? Time for a third try. The problem: I had only two eggs left.

Thank goodness DJ was there. He headed for HyVee, a twenty-five-minute round trip, and while he was gone, I scraped out the mixing bowl and rinsed the second batch down the drain. Then, it happened.

Water was standing in the sink, so I flipped on the garbage disposal, but dirty water just swirled around and around in the sink. I opened the cabinet doors underneath the sink to reset the garbage disposal, thinking it would be an easy fix. Much to my chagrin, the dirty water continued to just churn, going nowhere.

DJ got back with the eggs, saw my dilemma, and volunteered to do some plumbing. He lay on the floor and put his head inside the cabinet. He asked for a set of pliers and a bucket. He loosened the pipes and said, "Judy, you have banana peels clogging the pipe."

Who knew you weren't supposed to put banana peels down the garbage disposal?

When he removed the blockage, the disgusting water gushed down the drain and into the pan I had handed him earlier. He said, "Quick! I need another pan!" With no time to get another pan, I took the full one from him, and, knowing time was of the essence and employing some quick thinking, I instinctively poured the contents of the pan into the sink.

The first thing I noticed was that the drain was working fine now. Unfortunately, DJ's head was perfectly positioned underneath the sink and the uncoupled pipes.

I looked down to find his face soaked, his clothes sopping wet, the inside of the cabinet flooded, and the kitchen floor flooded. I cringed, knowing what had happened, and not knowing what to do or say. I just froze. Up to this point in our relationship, we had not shared a cross word with one another—not one. And here he was, dripping wet, covered in murky kitchen water, and wiping his face with his hands. Then suddenly, DJ who was still lying on his back on the floor, started laughing. Wild, hilarious laughter. And I did too.

I knelt down, handed him a towel and gave him a hug. "Darlin', you passed the test. I will definitely marry you."

Now that's what we call "A Judy Moment."

My third and final attempt to bake the cake went off like clockwork. I filled the three round cake pans with the right consistency batter and placed them in the very preheated oven to bake. Next came the creamed cheese and coconut frosting, which was made and set aside for the final step—assembling and icing the three layers once baked and cooled. With less than an hour remaining until the guests arrived, it was time to clean the kitchen, take a shower, and get dressed for the evening. I then opened a bottle of Cabernet Sauvignon to share a glass with my beloved partner ahead of the guests. A toast to DJ!

Oops! I suddenly realized it was only a few minutes before 6 p.m. I grabbed the lasagna pan from the fridge and placed it in the oven. With no time to spare, the guests arrived right on time. Lindy and her friends raved about the dinner and, most notably, the "fifteen-egg" Italian cream cake ... almost like the one my mother used to make. Delicious!

A Pearl of Wisdom:

Love Unconditionally

As in this "Judy Moment," love makes doing even the everyday, ordinary, and sometimes challenging tasks liberating for your soul. Love each other. Serve each other. Accept one another.

When you find a partner who loves and accepts you with all your "Judy Moments," you unlock the key to one's heart in spite of the other person's imperfections and shortcomings; it's more than just tolerating those embarrassing and awkward moments, which happen to all of us. It's about embracing someone's faults and weaknesses—big and small.

You may just find those occurrences can even lead to a source of joy and delight. When you can do that, you will discover a deeply felt unconditional love and an unbreakable, shatterproof bond that will get you through the more problematic challenges that come your way. Love unconditionally.

Oh, and remember: It's best not to put banana peels down the drain.

Photo Album

Our first portrait of our family of four.

Visiting my elementary school (now a museum) in White Cloud, Kansas.

Third date? ....
Or third anniversary?

Artist Robin John Anderson at his studio and gallery, Old Mingus Art Center, in Jerome, Arizona.

The day I said, "Yes ... a thousand times yes!"

At a niece's wedding in Texas.

One of our favorite activities ... preparing meals together.

Exchanging our wedding vows in front of Josh who officiated the ceremony.

With our family at the Lodge of Sedona on our wedding day.

My favorite DJ at the
height of his radio days.

So ...
who is this man?

Dinner in Boulder,
Colorado, the night
before I found out I had
cancer.

The Pink Brigade (Jordan, DJ, and Karen)
in the waiting room while I was in surgery.

Our cabin in the
woods setting before
groundbreaking.

Enjoying a fire and a glass
of wine at our new cabin
near Table Rock Lake.

On the Country Club Plaza in Kansas City with the street musician who dedicated a song to us during my breast-cancer journey.

At home in St. Joseph feeling stronger than ever.

Taking in the moment at Jordan and Ryan's wedding.

My retirement party with our family at emPowerU.

Hiking with Taylor to a Sinaqua ruins dating back to around A.D. 600.

Jan Sitts, the artist of Sedona at Sunset, in her studio at Sedona, Arizona (www.jansitts.com).

Enjoying a meal at Antico Forno Marucci in Rome, Italy.

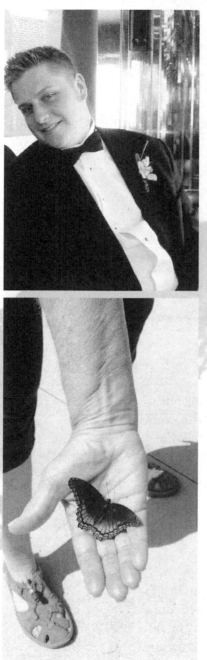

My son, Hayden (1991–2021).

A sign from above ... the black and blue butterfly.

Spending the day with our dear friends, Gary Marx (my editor) and his wife, Pam.

Enjoying one of our favorite wines in Napa Valley and toasting to life.

Sitting atop Brim's Mesa in Sedona reflecting on our many blessings and the possibilities for our future.

Chapter 8

So ... Who Is This Man?

FALLING IN LOVE WITH DJ was easy. In fact, it happened almost instantly. Everything my heart ever desired came true when I met this extraordinary man. The more I knew about him, the deeper our connection grew.

DJ—or Dennis, as most people call him—was raised in Fairfield, a community in southern Illinois. The town's population was about 6,000 at that time. As the middle child of Ivan and Bonnie Holler, DJ was sandwiched between a sister and a brother. It was a hard-working and deeply religious family.

Like many kids, DJ loved sports, biked to the community pool every day in the summer, and had his own paper route to earn a little spending cash. Living in small town America was the good life back then. These were the days before cell phones and computers, and everyone knew their neighbors. Fairfield was a safe place to raise a family. Oftentimes, DJ would leave home on his bike shortly after breakfast to join his friends for the day and return to his house right before the dinner bell sounded at 5 p.m.

DJ ran his paper route on bicycle two days a week for four years, knowing his "can't wait to get the local news" readers depended on him for delivering the paper like clockwork, regardless of the weather. Just like the postman, you were expected to show up through rain, sleet, snow, or sunshine.

During his freshman year at a nearby community college, he focused on a communications degree, which tied in to his longtime interest in radio. As an eighteen-year-old with no radio experience, he took a chance and applied for a part-time job as a disc jockey. When he got the job, it was like hitting the big time. While most of his friends were flipping burgers, putting curlicues on top of Dairy Queen ice cream cones, babysitting the neighbor's kids, or mowing yards, DJ was spinning records at the WFIW radio station in Fairfield. He played Top Forty tunes from 1971 to 1974, jumping to WJPS in nearby Salem and later to another station in Evansville, Indiana. His final listening audience consisted of over 100,000 who tuned in to hear the Voice.

One of DJ's biggest influences in his radio career was his dad's cousin, Merle Harmon, who started the

University of Kansas Jayhawk Sports Network and was one of two professional baseball sportscasters for the former Kansas City Athletics. Merle ended his career as an announcer on national television for college football and the play-by-play radio announcer for the Texas Rangers.

Realizing that very few make it into the major radio markets, and with the depressed salaries in the smaller markets, DJ decided to go another route. He pursued a business degree at a small private college in Iowa, while he worked to put himself through school. With his strong work ethic and drive, magnetic personality, deep humility, and integrity—and now with a business degree in hand—he landed a job as an underwriter in the commercial insurance business. That job would become a forty-year career, the last twenty-three years with Munich Re, an international reinsurance company. With his certified Chartered Property Casualty Underwriter (CPCU) designation, leadership skills, and a heart for serving, he held local, regional, and national volunteer positions, serving as president of the Kansas City CPCU chapter and later as a regional governor at the national level. He retired in 2018 as vice president with Munich Re.

He met his first wife, Pam, at a school event during his senior year in college. DJ had a bag of popcorn and noticed a pretty young woman sitting nearby. He saw his opening to meet her and offered to share his snack with Pam. This was the beginning of a thirty-seven-year relationship. After dating for several years, they married in 1978. Pam finished her nursing degree two years later. Their son, Ryan, came along in 1985.

Then, after thirty-one years of marriage, Pam was diagnosed with stage three cancer, and it quickly became stage four. Overnight their lives changed. They now spent most of their waking hours focused on Pam's health and well-being.

Colon cancer is a horrible disease. Facty Health cites colon cancer as "the third most commonly occurring form of cancer in the world, it usually begins with small, precancerous polyps, which may turn cancerous if they remain unchecked." According to WebMD, "Stage Four colon cancer has a relative five-year survival rate of about fourteen percent." This means that fewer than one out of seven people with this type of cancer are likely to still be alive five years after their diagnosis. Known to be a silent killer, sadly it's often too late once the disease is detected at this stage.

When Pam was diagnosed, her oncology doctors from Kansas City recommended major surgery, radiation, and chemotherapy. Even by following the medical experts' advice, they said Pam had a five percent chance of living another four years. The doctors gave her little to no chance of recovering. With such grim news, the couple carefully weighed their options and said "to hell with that."

DJ searched and found an internationally known naturopathic oncologist, Dr. Daniel Rubin, based in Scottsdale, Arizona. Dr. Rubin specializes in the integration of both conventional and naturopathic medicine for cancer patients. Many patients seek only the naturopathic care path if they cannot or choose not to go through conventional therapy. Because of the advanced stage of her disease, DJ and Pam were committed to the non-traditional route in hopes of finding a cure. Three annual trips of one week were made to the doctor's office in Arizona. Dr. Rubin also checked on Pam's condition and progress through monthly conference calls.

Heavy doses of vitamin C and herbal medicines were prescribed. Her treatment required injecting vitamin C into her blood stream on a daily basis. A port was placed in her chest so DJ could more easily administer the vitamin therapy at home.

Within the first year, the doctor suggested they seek experimental treatment abroad. Europe seemed to offer the best options, with the ongoing development of new protocols. These practices had yet to gain the Food and Drug Administration's (FDA) approval for use with cancer patients in the United States. The FDA goes through a rigorous, multi-year process before new treatments are approved. At that time, there were no Right to Try laws for terminally ill patients to seek experimental treatment.

The family made the first of three annual trips to Austria. Each trip lasted one to two weeks. The first experimental treatment involved heating cancer cells. The exploratory therapy required Pam to be placed in a chamber with heated blankets covering her body. Her body temperature was raised to a high degree to kill the cancer cells. Her care continued to be supplemented with high doses of vitamin C when they returned home.

During the last year that they sought care in Austria, a side trip was made to another cancer provider in Germany. The second experimental protocol removed white blood cells from Pam's body. Her blood was circulated through a machine. The white blood cells were spun out to energize and increase the cell count. The cells were then injected back into her body.

The European treatments slowed the progression of the disease and gave Pam a better quality of life. Eventually, however, reality set in. Even with the European treatments and vitamin therapy, the disease continued to slowly spread to other parts of her body. The family could not sustain a long-term treatment plan abroad.

DJ was working full time from home and limited his business travel in those first three years. He was Pam's primary caregiver. As her disease progressed, he stopped traveling all together so he could be with her while still working from home. Each day involved giving Pam IV treatments. The daily procedure would take up to three hours. As her care needs advanced, Ryan moved back home to help in the last months of his mother's life.

Pam's condition worsened, and she became weaker and weaker. The cancer had metastasized throughout her entire body. As a result of an emergency surgery, Pam was forced to wear a bag. As part of their new routine, DJ had to void and clean the pouch several times a day. Bathing and dressing his wife were other essential tasks he performed in addition to the household chores.

After Pam's surgery, the doctors in Kansas City suggested a bone marrow transplant.

After asking about the procedure and the potential benefits, they were told it might extend her life another sixty days or so. It was also made clear to them that the transplant procedure would not improve her quality of life. After some deep soul searching, DJ and Pam decided the procedure was simply out of the question.

The medical care needed was becoming overwhelming in Pam's last stage of life. Hospice care was called. In those last two months, the nurses and aides were there to help and comfort the family, and, most importantly, to assist Pam in the process of dying as peacefully as possible.

On her last day, Ryan and his fiancée, Mary Jo, were with DJ at Pam's bedside. They reminisced about their lives together and shared memories. Even though she was not able to respond, they felt certain that she heard every word, every story they told. Her sister Janet, brother-in-law Dave, and nephew Paul traveled from out-of-state to see her one last time and say goodbye. Soon after, Pam crossed over to enter heaven. Her grieving parents, Paul and Janet, came by a short time later to be with the family, and they mourned and prayed together.

After a lengthy battle, Pamela Kim Holler succumbed to cancer on April 7, 2012. During this journey,

DJ became more in tune with his spirituality and interested in learning more about life after death. He says Pam's struggle was a life-altering experience for him and helped him appreciate just how precious life is.

Ryan and Mary Jo were DJ's greatest supporters in his time of grief, as he was going through the motions of life, trying to just get by day to day. One year after his mom's passing, Ryan started to nudge his father back out into the world, to try to enjoy life once again.

Slowly, DJ took a few steps in that direction. He ruled out online dating, but he explored other sources and found a local, credible dating service. Like a typical underwriter, he appreciated the fact that the service did a careful review of every applicant to ensure each participant met their high standards. Besides an in-depth interview, applicants had to complete and pass psychological and mental testing, financial disclosures, and criminal background checks.

His matchmaker introduced him to a number of women who exhibited like-mindedness and shared his drive. They were strong, successful women, including doctors, entrepreneurs, nurses, psychologists, and other professionals who were smart, attractive, and confident. A few could have been good friends, yet something was missing. After nearly a dozen disappointing dates, it seemed there was no real connection, nor a reason to pursue a serious relationship.

Then, in June of 2013, DJ started bleeding internally.

He went to the doctor's office to explain his symptoms. The doctor said blood work needed to be done, but drawing the blood in the office would take several days to get the results back. He was then advised to go immediately to the nearest emergency room, which was located a few blocks away. Not grasping the urgency of the medical situation, he returned home to pack an overnight bag and shut down his computer. He made a few calls, including one to his boss in Princeton, New Jersey, to let him know he might not be at work the next day. After taking his time, he drove himself to a nearby medical center nearly an hour later.

He had difficulty walking from the car into the emergency room. His legs felt like they were on fire. He later found out the burning sensation was a result of the lack of blood circulation through his body. At the ER registration desk, he was pale as a ghost, had challenges with his breathing, and felt as if he could pass out. The hospital personnel recognized the urgency of his condition and swiftly wheeled him back to a treatment room.

Blood was promptly drawn and within minutes, the results confirmed internal hemorrhaging. The ER staff started to pump blood into his veins to keep him alive. He was moved to ICU. Over the next critical forty-eight hours, ten units of blood would be pumped into his body. A normal man has twelve units. DJ was literally on the verge of bleeding to death.

Meanwhile, the radiology team in the imaging room was trying to locate the source of the bleeding, and the standby medical team was prepared to do emergency surgery to save his life. He was told to lie still and not move. Doing so placed pressure on the site of the leak and the bleeding stopped. So, when the technician performed the scan, it was impossible to pinpoint the location.

DJ was sent back to ICU. And the bleeding began again. With timing of the essence, the medical transporter whisked him back to the imaging room to start another scan. Again, he was told to lie very still and not move. The result was the same. Nothing could be detected. The doctors were at a loss. He was returned to ICU, and again the hemorrhaging resumed. After two failed attempts, a decision was made to perform a colonoscopy, but there was too much blood. For a third time, he was placed on the gurney and rushed back to radiology.

DJ was conscious throughout the entire ordeal. At one point, one of the doctors calmly informed him, "We haven't found the location of the leak yet." At this time, DJ had no idea how close to death he was.

He vividly recalled the episode: "As the tech began each of the procedures, I was told to lie very still and not move. Only on the third imaging scan procedure, something quite different was happening. As I lay there, the entire treatment room turned a deep blue. The color was so brilliant that words cannot describe its beauty. Then, all of a sudden, I saw a tiny crystal-clear light appear. It continued to grow and expand larger and larger as if a tunnel were opening up."

He said he could feel himself being drawn out of his physical body toward the light.

"At that moment, I felt an inner calmness and complete peace. Understanding what was happening, I could have easily gone through the tunnel to cross over into heaven. But just as quickly, I thought of Ryan. What kind of impact would it have on this young man's life—an only child—if I chose to leave? After all, his mother had passed away only a year or so earlier. Then, I thought, 'God, I'm not ready to go, not yet.' I shifted my body and the movement caused the bleeding to start. Almost instantly, the radiology technician yelled, 'I found it!' The tunnel abruptly disappeared, and I was back in my own consciousness."

DJ was quickly transported to a pre-op room to be prepped for emergency surgery with not a moment to spare. The surgeon marked his abdomen with a black marker, explaining, "If we are forced to remove most of your colon, we will have to place a bag on you."

"No bag!"

DJ was adamant. Pam's suffering the final months of her life, the indignity she felt about wearing the bag, was still fresh in his mind. But the doctor insisted, "We'll do it if we need to save your life."

"You do not have my permission. No bag!"

The doctor continued to mark his abdomen and then left the pre-op room. As soon as he was gone, DJ rubbed off the markings.

Following the procedure, the surgeon told DJ that one and a half feet of colon had to be removed to fix the leak. Fortunately, attaching a bag was not necessary. Not out of the woods yet, DJ remained in the intensive care unit for three weeks and on the general patient floor for another week. He was finally discharged from the hospital after thirty days, weighing thirty pounds lighter. In his first follow-up visit, the surgeon said, "We thought we were going to lose you."

That's when it became clear how close he was to dying; it caused him to re-examine his existence even more closely. Since Pam's death, he had just been going through the motions of daily living. Experiencing this second life-altering event, it became clear he wanted to embrace life to the fullest.

His attitude for meeting new people changed, and he was ready to live and love again. Spending the month of July recovering, he completed the physical healing process and began his new journey in being alive in this world.

In August, I showed up.

It was definitely a "God thing" when we met. Common interests, same values, love for family and friends, life-changing events in our lives, spiritually grounded, and career-driven. Each of us was passionate about life and filled with an attitude of gratitude.

I believe I was introduced to DJ when we were both ready. What a blessing it is to have met this extraordinary guy. So, who is this man? Truly, this man is my soul twin.

A Pearl of Wisdom:
Embrace Life to the Fullest

Living your life to the fullest is contrary to what many people may think. Some would say it applies to only experiencing good things. Actually, I believe it can happen in many ways regardless of what your current situation is or past circumstances have been. Even when you face pain, sadness, illness, and/or loss, you can dig deep within your soul to find an appreciation for life and living. Living fully means you embrace all of life, which includes how you gratefully appreciate the good times as well as how you face the more challenging ones.

In all situations, you have the opportunity to learn and grow. Sometimes that means you must unlearn what you've learned to fully heal your heart, your body, and your soul. If you tap into your inner guidance and live by faith, you can reinvigorate your life with an abundance of healing, joyfulness, serenity, and love.

As DJ says: "When life gets tough, which will happen, you have a choice. You can approach the situation with love, humility, and gratitude or with bitterness and a victim mentality. I choose to embrace life with love. Live life to the fullest."

Chapter 9

Sedona at Dusk

DJ AND I WERE eager to announce to our families and friends that we were getting married in five months. While still on our trip in Arizona, we began to make wedding plans. We agreed that an outdoor wedding at the place we were staying, The Lodge of Sedona, would be perfect.

It's called a lodge, but it is really a majestic bed and breakfast. Its impeccably manicured grounds had a Zen-like feel, with a rose garden and pools of water, massive evergreens, native plants and shrubs, artistic wind sculptures, and Frank Lloyd Wright-inspired elements. There was a rock labyrinth and another circular path with Native American features, and the gigantic Red Rock formations provided a dramatic backdrop for the entire scene. From the very moment we walked onto these grounds, we felt a spiritual connection resonating deep within our souls.

A private ceremony was set for June 14, 2014. We decided to keep it small and intimate, with only our children and their spouses present to witness. Lisa, the manager of the bed and breakfast, helped us make the arrangements. We asked her if she could recommend both a minister and a photographer from the area. She offered the names of several people she knew who could officiate. One of the people she recommended, Josh, was a young man we had met that first night in Sedona.

It was late when we arrived at the lodge that first night, and no one was there to greet us. But there was a small library table with a dimly lit lamp and a welcome sign. Propped against the lamp was a sealed envelope with DJ's name on it. It contained a letter of greeting, a set of keys, and a card with the number of our suite. We had absolutely no idea where to go, and there appeared to be a dozen or so guest rooms spread throughout the sprawling two-story inn. So, we ventured out and explored the main floor on our own.

There was a large open kitchen and a living room area with soft lighting and Mission-style furniture, including a leather couch with billowy pillows. Native American patterns were prominent, and it was a welcoming, comfortable space. Beyond this room were two other common areas: a guest dining room with eight or so tables and a family room that contained a TV, library shelves, and books.

Just as we were contemplating what we should do, this tall, lanky, and almost ghostly figure stepped out of the back hallway. He introduced himself as Josh.

He was in his late twenties or early thirties, very attractive with long dark hair pulled behind his ears and held in place by a do-rag. When he greeted us, it was immediately apparent he possessed a gentle and kind spirit. It was as if he, with his calm demeanor and quiet voice, had stepped out of a time when hippies made love and protested the war.

Josh had stayed late to prepare juices and other breakfast items for guests the next morning. Among the many hats he wore at the lodge was the one he wore as sous chef. He took time to give us a tour of the rest of the facility that night and shared information about his favorite hiking trails and other points of interest. He made us feel at home then escorted us to our suite.

Over the course of our stay, we seemed to bond at a level you wouldn't expect to form with a sous chef and juicer. Each evening after we returned from a day of hiking and sightseeing, we'd see Josh and he would ask about our day. And we would ask about his. Our conversations were not simple small talk. He was genuinely interested in us, as we were in him.

Besides being a lodge for out-of-town guests like us, the facility provides residential health and wellness care for people with cancer. Josh gave support, comfort, and a sense of hope to those going through the healing process. It was readily apparent Josh had a real passion for that aspect of his job. It was a calling in his life.

Given all of his talents and interests, it shouldn't have surprised us to learn that another hat Josh wore was that of an ordained minister. It seemed like icing on the wedding cake. DJ and I agreed to ask him the next day. We did, and he heartily accepted.

Now we needed a photographer. Lisa suggested a few studios in the area, and the first couple I called were already booked for the date we'd chosen in June. It did not look promising, and I was getting concerned. We cast a wider net. Aniron Photography was in a small rural community, about a thirty-minute drive from Sedona. When I called, the woman who answered declined without hesitation, insisting her studio specialized in photo shoots of pregnant women and mothers with their newborns.

I told her our situation, explaining it would be a small wedding with only our children and their spouses present. She paused, and it seemed like she was thinking it over. Then she said, "In that case, yes. You can count on me to be there." Yes!

Five months passed quickly. DJ and I arrived back in Sedona a few days before the kids to finalize our plans. First, we had to get our marriage license in Camp Verde. With only a few couples ahead of us, obtaining the license went smoothly.

Now back in Sedona, Uptown was our next stop. Momentarily, we went our separate ways. I browsed inside a small boutique, while DJ headed to another shop. I purchased three red beaded bracelets for Jordan, Kristen, and Mary Jo. I also found Native American arrowheads from another shop for DJ, the three Ryans, and Hayden.

Our children arrived at different times on Thursday, and, after they settled in, the family cruised through and shopped in Uptown, the Tlaquepaque Square, and other notable places that afternoon. We grabbed dinner at a popular Mexican restaurant named Javelina Cantina where we also enjoyed spectacular views.

A scenic Red Rocks hot air balloon ride had been arranged for the family to lift off at sunrise on the morning of our wedding day. Kristen and I had to pass on the balloon ride. She was six months pregnant, and I had had a nasty fall a few months earlier. Both were conditions that restricted us from going on the adventure. Instead, we decided to treat ourselves to relaxing massages.

The balloon ride had to be canceled, though, because it was so windy that morning, so DJ and the rest of the family booked an off-road adventure with Pink Jeep Tours. The tour took them along Sedona's Broken Arrow Trail. This new escapade gave them a chance to capture the breath-taking panoramic views of the Red Rocks formations by land. Afterward, we all headed to The Secret Garden Café for an early lunch. After eating, we ventured through the shops and galleries in the Tlaquepaque Square.

Around four o' clock, we went back to the bed and breakfast to get ready for the wedding, which was set for 7 p.m., or just around dusk. Jordan came to my suite to help me get ready, while DJ went to Ryan and Mary Jo's suite to dress. With little time to prepare, I rehearsed my thoughts over and over in my head, contemplating what I wanted to say in vowing my steadfast love and devotion to this man I would soon marry.

Prior to the wedding, our photographer took photos in the rose garden where the ceremony was to take place. She photographed me in my red sleeveless Kate Spade dress and Jordan, Kristen, and Mary Jo in their black dresses. Then it was the guys' turn with DJ in a black suit with white open-collared shirt and my sons, Ryan and Hayden, and DJ's Ryan, and Jordan's Ryan—all dressed in white, open-collared shirts and black slacks.

Just before the ceremony, I asked Jordan to deliver a wedding card and a small gift to DJ. The present was a red tie for DJ to wear with his white shirt and black suit. I must admit I had a bit of pre-wedding jitters, but I knew unquestionably that this was the man I wanted to spend the rest of my life with.

With the sun setting and the Red Rocks in the background, my two sons each took one arm and walked me out the front doors of the lodge onto the patio to the steps leading down to the rose garden. A ten-foot-tall wind sculpture whirled in the gentle breeze. Down the patio steps stood DJ. He flashed a huge smile as his big bright eyes sparkled.

Josh officiated the wedding. After a few words, he asked us to share our vows.

I tend to be more spontaneous and do better when I speak from my heart rather than from a scripted speech, so the written record of my vows are not reliable. But this is what I recall saying that day:

DJ, I remember the first time we met on a Friday night in August. You texted to let me know you had arrived early and were waiting for me in the courtyard. You wrote that you had arranged a band for our very first date. I recall laughing out loud as I parked my car to meet you for the very first time. I said to myself, "I love this man," recognizing that you had a sense of humor. Bands always play on Second Friday Nights.

It was so easy to be with you from the moment we met.

I love your smiling eyes. Your sense of humor. Your kindness. Our deep spiritual connection. The way you embrace each moment of every day. I love the way you look at me and the way you love me.

You are my soul twin. I am so blessed to have found you and share the last trimester of our lives together.

DJ, you truly are my forever love!

DJ followed and shared these words that he had carefully jotted down:

Judy, you have changed my life.
   We are connected in a way that
   Goes beyond friendship, beyond romance.
   We are connected on the soul level.

My spirit is lifted when I am with you.
The sound of your voice,
The way you laugh,
You have brought joy back into my life.
I promise to love you always,
To honor you
And to cherish you.
I not only love you,
I am in love with you.
You are my Lady in Red
Forever and Always.

Josh then declared us "husband and wife." And we kissed.

One of the last pictures our photographer captured was the two of us standing in the center of the labyrinth. This circular footpath symbolizes that you are on a spiritual journey and exactly where you are meant to be. Labyrinth walking has also been described as an ancient practice used by many different faith walkers to quiet their minds and focus on spiritual contemplation or prayer. On June 14, 2014, God answered our prayers.

Before the photographer left, she thanked us for including her. "It's been such a blessing to be a part of your special day," she said. The next day, among the beautiful photographs of new and expectant mothers and babies on her website—at the top center of her page—was a photo of DJ and me in the middle of the labyrinth, embracing each other with a gentle kiss. Beneath the photo were these words: "Sometimes in the labyrinth of life, we travel far and wide, when suddenly we find our soul mate in the center."

To this day, when we make our annual trek to Sedona, we enter the circular path individually in deep contemplation, meditation, and prayer. It is a time to renew our commitment to one another, living life fully, and embracing our faith in God. We then join hands in the center of the labyrinth and quietly walk out together.

That evening, our family celebrated with dinner at Dahl and Di Luca Ristorante Italiano. DJ and I made a reservation a day or two earlier, letting the maître d' know we were getting married on that day. When we arrived, the restaurant staff had a special place set up for our family, which they had secretly decorated with white candles, fresh flowers, and scattered red rose petals down the middle of the large rectangular table. After we were seated, our kids toasted to our new life together.

As best man, Ryan Holler talked about his dad and I finding each other and how happy he was for the two of us. He mentioned how lonely his dad had been until we met, and he thanked me for saving his dad's life. Truth be known, his dad saved my life, too.

Jordan, as my maid of honor, gave us a notebook for DJ and me to record our love story. She filled the first few pages with her own message, which included a piece of scripture:

"We have this hope as an anchor for the soul, firm and secure."— Hebrews 6:19 (NIV)

She added these words: *"Hope is a great word that we hold near and dear to our hearts. I have to tell you my heart is at peace, now that you've found your soul mate. I have been hoping and praying for this moment, ever since I can remember."*

The following spring, DJ and I returned to Sedona, which will always be a sacred place for us. We found peace on the hiking trails and enjoyed restaurants and shopping in Tlaquepaque Square. As we browsed through one of the Rene Taylor art galleries, DJ and I stopped suddenly before a stunning abstract painting. It took our breath away. Somehow it perfectly captured our wedding day, evoking the sandstone formations with brilliant purple, red, gold, and orange hues as if illuminated by the sun. We admired it for a long time and moved closer to see the name of the artist and the title of the piece. It was called *Sedona at Dusk* by Jan Sitts. Looking closer, we both imagined what appeared to be the image of an angel superimposed on the painting. We left the gallery, but that work of art did not leave our minds.

After we got back home, and without DJ knowing, I called the gallery and purchased *Sedona at Dusk*. I presented it to him on our first anniversary. It is now hanging in our living room.

A Pearl of Wisdom:

Celebrate Life

For DJ and me, celebrating life has been found in precious little moments. Savor those times, big or small. They could be found on a hike that connects you to nature or while pausing to view the splendor of a sunset. They could pour forth at a gathering of family—at a wedding in Sedona. Or elsewhere. Those precious moments might also be discovered in a gallery through a piece of art.

The spirit of celebration will take root in your heart when you purposefully seek it out. Take the time to celebrate in quiet gratitude, or with triumphant jubilation, for the many blessings you receive. Most likely, those remembrances will touch your life forever.

Chapter 10

Stand by Me

AFTER A BRUTAL DIVORCE and then being alone the next twelve years, I had finally met the man of my dreams and was living the most joyful time of my life. Just ninety-three days after DJ and I married, however, life was about to suddenly change again.

In September of 2014, I was scheduled for a mammogram as a follow-up to an MRI procedure I had six months earlier. The MRI results were clear, but the radiologist suggested a mammogram simply as a precaution.

I was very familiar with the Mosaic Life Care's Outpatient Center in Plaza One, not only because of the medical care I had received there, but because of my work. I knew dozens of people in this building, had participated in leadership meetings with them, sat on boards and committees with them, and socialized with some at community events. I was on a first-name basis with many of them.

After a short wait, Cindy, my radiology technician, greeted me warmly and escorted me back to the imaging room. She handed me a hospital gown and left while I changed. I waited in the cold, sterile room for her to return. Once she did, she completed the imaging scans in a matter of minutes. She left the room to give the images to the radiologist to make an assessment.

All of this was fairly routine. What normally happens is that the radiologist gives the green light, the technician gives me the good news, and I get dressed and go back to work. But this time was different. Cindy returned and told me the radiology physician would like to meet with me.

I hurriedly dressed, nervously wondering what might be wrong. She escorted me down the hallway to the doctor's office. The scans were lit up on the screen, and, after the doctor greeted me and we talked for a short while, he pointed to the images. He drew my attention to an area of my left breast.

He said the images showed a couple of masses, and there was a high probability it was cancer. His explanation was detailed, but it wasn't sinking in. My mind was racing. What I did hear the doctor say was another test was needed, this time a core biopsy. The procedure was scheduled for the next day.

I left the room in a fog wondering what had just happened. At the same time, I felt somewhat confident that everything would be okay, if past experience was any guide. I had two close encounters some years earlier when self-examinations detected lumps in my breast. In both cases, my surgeon recommended I have a lumpectomy to remove the abnormal tissue. It's considered a breast conserving surgery to excise only the tumor and the margins around it—unlike a mastectomy, which removes the entire breast. After each of the lumpectomies, which were some years apart, the pathology reports indicated the tumors were benign.

The surgeon did indicate I had a condition called atypical hyperplasia. The Mayo Clinic defines atypical hyperplasia as a precancerous condition that causes an accumulation of abnormal cells in the breast. It isn't cancer, but it can be a forerunner to cancer. Before I left my post-surgery appointment from my first lumpectomy that day, the surgeon informed me it was quite likely this issue might occur again. As a precaution, he also declared how important annual mammograms would be for the rest of my life. I faithfully complied.

Now years after that visit, I felt somewhat confident this would be no different from the biopsy results from the other two times. Even though my own mother battled breast cancer in her early twenties, I believed the tumors buried deep in my chest were benign.

Cancer was something my mother never talked about— ever. In fact, she seemed to be in denial that she had ever had the disease, and it haunted this strong, independent woman all of her adult life. It was hard for me to imagine. She was in her early twenties and a new bride. Her life was just starting!

Grandmother Legler, Mom's mom, took me into her confidence and told me about it when I was a junior in high school. She said Mom had discovered a lump in her breast shortly after marrying my dad. Mom had a radical mastectomy followed by radiation treatments. My grandmother knew how difficult it was for Mom and figured she would never talk with me about it, but she thought it was important for me to know.

Living in a small rural area in northeast Kansas at that time, Mom was somewhat shunned by her friends and the community because of her battle with cancer, my grandmother explained. Back then, in the late 1940s, people referred to cancer as "the Big C," and many people thought it was contagious.

It was also a time before medical personnel suggested major breast reconstruction as part of the medical treatment and emotional healing process. In those days, you wore a breast prothesis with a specially designed bra to make you look as normal as possible after breast removal.

My mother was a very proud and private woman, and this was a burden she carried the rest of her life. The only time she brought it up to me was shortly before I married my first husband, and she did so hesitantly. We were out shopping in preparation for my wedding day, set for January 31. I remember sitting with her in a restaurant as we stopped for an iced tea. As she spoke about her ordeal, her voice quivered and tears streamed down her face.

She said she felt robbed. After the doctor completed her surgery to remove the lump from her breast, she was kept under anesthetic while the specimen was sent to pathology to be examined. It was definitely cancer.

Mom said that while she was still under, the surgeon met with my dad and Mom's parents in the waiting room to give them the news. The doctor explained that Bertha's best chance for survival was a total mastectomy to completely remove her breast.

Later, she was told that my father—also in his early twenties—was absolutely terrified and heartbroken for his new bride's fate. He left the room in tears, leaving the decision to my grandparents. They gave the surgeon permission to amputate, acknowledging that the doctor and his team should do what was necessary to save their daughter's life.

Her hands visibly shaking, my precious mother disclosed the horrible day that was deeply etched in her mind as if it were yesterday. She was waking up in the recovery room, slowly coming out of the anesthetic, when the doctor gave her the news, "Bertha, I'm sorry to tell you this, but you have cancer, and we had to remove your breast."

Mom said she felt cheated that she wasn't given the opportunity to make the decision for herself. She never accepted the fact that she ever had cancer. After more than several decades of hiding her secret, she was now releasing her emotionally scarring agony to her twenty-eight-year-old daughter. I cannot even begin to imagine how difficult it was for her to share this still unbearable, life experience with me.

On the day of my biopsy, I found myself sitting alone and nervous, waiting to be called in for the procedure, and I could not stop thinking about Mom's battle with breast cancer. I wondered if I too had "the Big C." As I sat there praying, all of a sudden, I felt a *swoosh* go through my entire body. It was as if Mom, who had passed away some two years earlier, was letting me know she was there with me.

The radiology technician called my name and escorted me to the treatment room. The doctor explained the core needle biopsy procedure. With this type of diagnostic technique, the area is anesthetized locally with lidocaine. A small incision is made so a large needle can be inserted into the mass. Ultrasound provides guidance on the location of the targeted mass.

I was told to expect to feel pressure, tugging, dis-comfort, and then pain as a spring-loaded instrument captured a sample of tissue. Because the tumors were buried deep and the lidocaine only numbed the surface of my chest, the elongated core needle caused excru-ciating pain as the core samples were obtained. They collected six or eight samples. I felt like screaming. Finally, a marker was placed in the location of the mass so it could be easily found in case a future surgery was required. The outpatient procedure took approximately thirty minutes.

Following the procedure on Friday morning, the doctor said I would receive a call from the nurse practitioner from the Mosaic Breast Center once the results were confirmed. Now it was just a matter of waiting.

DJ and I flew to Colorado on Sunday. For twenty-some years, I had participated in a number of Kaiser Institute learning collaboratives: The Philanthropy Institute, Bliss, and Two Worlds Wisdom Gathering. Once again, the collaborative would be held at the Colorado Chautauqua in Boulder. Lee Kaiser, the Institute's founder and my mentor, is recognized as a health futurist and intuitive. He talks openly about spirituality. A deeply religious man, Lee looks at the world through a different lens. Instead of a world of scarcity, he sees a world of abundance. It's sort of like seeing the glass half full or half empty. It is what you make of it. For Lee, clearly the glass was nearly filled to the brim.

After checking in at the Chautauqua and settling into our cottage below the Flatirons, we strolled through downtown Boulder, exploring some boutiques and art galleries. We enjoyed dinner and shared a bottle of wine before heading back to the cabin. We talked and laughed, and both of us were excited about the next three days at the Wisdom School. But clearly, at the top of our minds, we were anxiously awaiting the news of the biopsy.

Before going to bed, we sat on the small screened-in porch, snuggled up to one another on what was a cool September evening. It just felt so safe and comforting to be in his arms. We sometimes read books to one another. After each chapter, we stop to interpret and comprehend what was just read. This night we were flicking through the pages and reading from a book we had started a week or so earlier. The book was *Answers About the Afterlife* by Bob Olson. The author, "a former skeptic and longtime private investigator," wrote about his fifteen-year research to uncover "the mysteries of life after death." His father's passing prompted him to search for the answers of what happens to us beyond this lifetime.

Exhausted from the weight on our shoulders, we closed the book and decided to retire for the night. I struggled to sleep wondering what the days and months ahead might hold for us. Surely, this was all just a bad dream.

The next morning, we walked a block to the Chautauqua's Community Learning Center, where the main room, with its Arts and Crafts motif, had been adorned with lighted candles, round pots of blooming mums, and flowering orchids along with various rocks and crystals atop the stone fireplace mantel. Pieces of artwork that had been created for the Institute over the years were resting on easels all around the room.

About 100 folding chairs were arranged in neat rows for seminar attendees. The familiar surroundings were calming to be in once again, and it was most uplifting to see old friends and the Kaiser family (Lee;

his wife, Betty; his grown children, Leanne and Kevin; their spouses, John and Michelle; and their longtime family friend and business associate Linda Scolin). As soon as I entered this familiar space, I felt a deep sense of relief and peace.

The day was enlightening with the gathering's core topic on "the wisdom law of love." In Lee's opening, he talked about "love as the basis of all attraction in the universe—what holds everything together." It seemed like the perfect topic for DJ and me as we were both focused on holding everything together in our lives at that moment.

Over the lunch hour, we signed up to have dinner at The Kitchen on Pearl Street with a small group of friends and a few new acquaintances. Shortly after the Institute adjourned for the day, DJ and I trekked back to our cottage to take a break before joining our dinner group. Once again, we sat on the screened-in porch and took turns reading to each other the next chapter or two of *Answers About the Afterlife.*

Then at 5:15 p.m., my cell phone rang. The call had an 816 area code, and my heart jumped. It was from Mosaic Life Care. I answered and immediately recognized Stacie's voice. She is the advanced nurse practitioner.

"Judy, I thought you would be okay, but the test results show you have breast cancer. I'm so sorry." She said a few more things, but not much sank in. All I heard was "breast cancer." I had "The Big C." It was Monday, September 15.

Stacie said she would set up appointments for me to meet in the next day or two with an oncologist, a radiologist, a general surgeon, and a plastic surgeon. I thought, why a plastic surgeon? I simply couldn't take it all in.

I was stunned, frozen, and scared beyond words. I had just married the love of my life and soul twin ninety-three days earlier. How could this be?

I walked out to the screened-in porch where DJ was sitting on the wicker settee. He put the book down on top of the wooden coffee table and looked straight at me. I just stood there. He haltingly said, "So...you don't have cancer. Right?"

I stood there not able to utter a word, shaking my head back and forth. His face changed. He was puzzled, concerned. "So, everything's alright?!"

I continued to shake my head, still not able to speak. He blurted out, "Tell me you're alright, sweetheart!" A tear started to roll down my cheek.

"DJ, I have breast cancer."

He jumped up, buried his head in his hands, and sobbed. "Judy, I don't think I can do this again."

I knew what he must be feeling. He was scared as much as I was. His first wife died two and a half years earlier of colon cancer after fighting it for three and a half years. The thought of losing his second wife was more than he could bear.

We held each other tightly and wept uncontrollably in each other's arms. Finally, we stopped crying and silently held each other for some time. Once we composed ourselves, we talked about the need to see the cancer specialists ASAP to discuss my options.

We called the restaurant and asked the hostess to let the group know we had a change in plans for the evening and would not be joining them. Instead, we ambled around the streets and sidewalks in Chautauqua Park. Trekking up the hill, we turned on Astor Lane where I noticed my good friend Eileen Zorn and her husband, Steve. They were just getting out of their car, ready to head to their cottage. It was the first time since arriving at the Wisdom Gathering that the two of us had a chance to speak with one another.

Eileen, one of the Kaiser guest faculty members for the Wisdom Gathering, is recognized as a heart-based leader and known for her compassion and commitment to service. No coincidence that Eileen was the first person I ran into after getting the frightful news that evening.

Eileen knew my life-changing stories, about my divorce and my parents' deaths. When she saw DJ and me, she beamed, hugged me, and asked how I was. I whispered in her ear, "I just found out that I have breast cancer." She held me tightly as tears welled up in her eyes and mine.

Eileen invited us to come into their bungalow to talk. DJ and I sat on the sofa in the living room as Steve and Eileen listened with calm compassion. Eileen asked if we wanted her to set up a time for DJ and me to talk privately with Lee the next morning. Yes, of course, we agreed. She also volunteered to arrange a gathering of some of the Kaiser attendees to be a part of a sacred healing circle before we left Boulder.

DJ and I left Eileen and Steve's place and strolled hand in hand back to the cabin, knowing we needed to call our children and a couple of close friends to share the news. Barely able to speak, I somehow managed to get the words out, "I have breast cancer." Needless to say, the conversations were tearful for all of us.

After a restless night, we arrived at the Wisdom Gathering on time the next morning. Eileen had arranged time after lunch for DJ and me to visit privately with Lee. In a quiet corner of the Chautauqua's Community Center, my dear friend met with us, and one of the first things he said with obvious love, kindness, and compassion was, "Judy, I didn't see this coming."

A two-decades-long friend and my life coach, Lee has been one of the most impactful people in my life. As a spiritual guide, a mentor, an intuitive, and a trusted friend, he has helped to shape my life and how I experience the world around me. Lee suggested that if DJ and I could financially afford to retire, we should do so right away. It was as if he was saying we should get our affairs in order. I felt grave concern in his voice that suggested he sensed a not so promising outcome.

Lee asked if he could offer a prayer. Having said yes, he had us turn around with our backs toward him. He gently placed his hands—one hand on my shoulder and the other on DJ's—and prayed a special blessing for us and our healing. After he repeated the words,

"So be it. Amen," a few times, we turned to face him. Lee said, "As I touched both of you, I noticed that your hearts beat as one."

Lee acknowledged how close we are to one another, not just as soul mates, but like "unusually rare" soul mates. We shared with him that several people have called us twin flames or soul twins. He confirmed a deep spiritual connection exists between us.

Lee promised he would keep us in his prayers. The realization was beginning to set in—we had a long arduous and uncertain journey ahead of us.

On our last day in Boulder and the conclusion of the retreat, Eileen brought together Wisdom Gathering friends and several new acquaintances to form a sacred circle. DJ and I sat in the center. The circle included a musician who played the harp, an abstract artist, a doctor, a counselor, and other faith walkers—all known as deeply spiritual people.

The healing space was in front of a calming water feature with a gentle waterfall flowing out of a four-foot boulder surrounded by large pine trees. The sun radiated down on us.

Each person shared life-affirming words. During those sacred moments, Eileen, from Loma Linda, California, led the group in a powerful healing encounter. Julie played the harp; Carol, the artist from Crested Butte, gifted us with two healing mandalas that she had created for people who are battling cancer; Karen, the LA physician, laid her healing hands on me; Margo, from South Bend, Indiana, represented the mother energy; Molly provided her kind words of wisdom and support; and John, from Brighton, Colorado, and a cancer survivor, concluded with a fervent prayer.

Their words and actions touched my heart. Tears welled up in my eyes and my whole body shook as I embraced this moment and what this small community did for us. I accepted their gift with deep gratitude. Then, suddenly, I felt complete calmness and serenity.

What took place in those moments were life affirming—a transformational moment—and it marked the beginning of my breast cancer journey. I felt empowered. I felt loved. I felt ready to face the biggest challenge of my life.

DJ and I acknowledged that we were taking a divergent path—an unknown path—filled with hope, some trepidation, and a sense of peace. We were ready to begin our new, unplanned journey to fight the battle together with God and our guardian angels by our side.

I have a heart filled with gratitude for Lee, Eileen, Julie, Carol, Karen, Margo, Molly, John, and the others who joined the circle to stand by me that day. And, of course, to DJ.

We left the Boulder area that afternoon with a feeling of joy and love, gratitude, and hope for our future together. The fear had subsided some, and we were ready to fight this thing. Honestly, there was no better place to get such devastating news than where we were, in that "oasis of respite, rejuvenation, and enlightenment." Clearly, we were surrounded by deep love, friendship, inspiration, and a sense of healing. It was not a coincidence we were in this special place.

Months earlier, we had made plans to leave the Kaiser Institute gathering in Boulder and fly directly to Anaheim, California, where DJ's professional association, the Charter Property and Casualty Underwriters, was holding its annual convention. I had taken vacation time to be with him, and I planned to accompany him to some of the functions. We did not alter those plans.

The convention was at the downtown Marriott Hotel, and, as we were getting ready to go to a reception and dinner that evening, I turned on Pandora radio so I could listen to music while I showered. When I finished, I stepped out of the shower and the song *Stand by Me* by Ben E. King came on. Dripping wet, I grabbed my favorite DJ, and we danced in our hotel room to the song. The lyrics resonated:

When the night is come/and the land is dark/and the moon is the only light we'll see/No I won't be afraid/Oh I won't be afraid/Just as long as you stand by me/If the sky that we look upon/should crumble and fall/or the mountain should crumble to the sea/I won't cry, I won't cry/No I won't shed a tear/Just as long as you stand, stand by me.

There was no doubt in my mind. None! I was quite

certain, in spite of all the uncertainty we faced, that DJ would "stand by me," and we would get through this frightening cancer journey together. The fight was on!

A Pearl of Wisdom:

Find Your Circle

My pastor, Adam Hamilton, just recently shared this message in his Sunday sermon: No matter what the adversity is that you experience in your life, don't give up. Persevere.

For DJ and me, the first week after getting the breast cancer diagnosis set the tone for this new unplanned, divergent path we were suddenly taking. From the very beginning, we recognized just how blessed we were to have deeply caring and compassionate friends who surrounded us with love in a sacred circle at the Colorado Chautauqua that cool autumn day in September. Clearly, love reverberated deep inside and made it possible for us to see into each other's souls.

In your own personal circumstances, create a sacred circle when faced with adversity. Your circle may be filled with family and friends who offer their love, concern, kindness, and support. You might find your circle includes only one special person who lifts you up. It's also conceivable that you find guidance or learn from someone else's experience in dealing with a similar challenge. Your circle just might be filled with your faith, and it will grasp the divine presence of God wrapped around you.

When you are alone—and you will feel alone and distracted at times—quiet your mind and listen for your inner voice. Be ready to boldly move forward in faith and have the courage to fight on.

Chapter 11

Decision Point

Now NEARLY FIVE YEARS *after getting my breast cancer diagnosis, the fear and anxiety of wondering what lay ahead had been pushed far away. I knew these chapters would be the most difficult to write about. I sorted through all the materials and notes I had gathered throughout my cancer journey, and, as I contemplated on how to begin writing, the raw emotions rose up inside of me.*

An hour or so later, DJ came up to the loft, my sacred writing space in our getaway cabin at south-west Missouri's Table Rock Lake. He sat in one of the oversized chairs and chatted for a minute or two, not realizing the dark place I was in. I stood up from my desk and went over to him. I kissed him multiple times in rapid succession with my eyes closed ever so tightly. I knew if I opened them, a flood of tears would flow. I couldn't speak. Quickly turning my back to him, I sat down at my desk as he continued to talk. Still not hearing a word he said, I continued to swallow hard to fight back the waterworks. I hid my emotions in that moment, not wanting him to know my mind was elsewhere.

Then I heard him ask if I wanted to take a boat ride. It seemed like the perfect escape from the haunting place I was in. We worked together to pre-pare the boat for an afternoon voyage, unsnapping the metal fasteners to release and roll up the canvas and uncover our twenty-four-foot Cobalt Runabout known as Olive Oyl. It was a perfect Saturday after-noon with the sun shining and the temperature in the mid-eighties. Dozens of boats were on the lake pulling skiers, water boarders, lake surfers, and tubers. It was a casual and carefree summer day, and we glided over the crystal-clear water, listening to Phil Collins' A Groovy Kind of Love.

DJ pulled into a favorite cove, a place we call Paradise. Only a few other boats were anchored there. We found a quiet place, and DJ dropped the anchor and came over to sit beside me. Phil Collins had become melancholy, and we listened to Against All Odds (Take A Look at Me Now). Still not able to shake the emotions, I broke down, and the held-back tears streaked down my face. At first, I could not utter a word. I suddenly realized I had been holding onto *these feelings all these years, throughout my cancer journey.*

Over the decades and with a lot of soul searching, I had learned to not dwell on things, but, for whatever reason, I couldn't pretend that they didn't happen. Now I was feeling the trepidation and sadness as if they were new. I tried to explain to DJ in as few words as possible what was going on with me. I could no longer bury it inside of me. I continued to turn away the onslaught of tears over and over again. Somehow, I recognized I had to once more fully embrace it. Once more I had to relive the most difficult part of my life's trek—facing cancer.

After several hours on the lake, I am now back in the cabin sitting at my writing desk. I again attempt to put into words and describe this life-altering slice of my journey. I did not choose this path; it chose me. So let me begin.

I was reliving my mother's nightmare. Early on, it dawned on me that she also was just newly married when she received her breast cancer diagnosis. I now fully understood the grave uncertainty she too must have felt in facing this dreaded disease.

On Sunday, September 21, 2014, we left sunny California and made our way back home to the KCI airport. DJ held my hand on the plane, and for most of the flight home we were immersed in our own thoughts.

All I could think about was this battle that now faced us. I can only imagine what must have been running through his mind.

Even though we were married, we maintained two homes, and we lived apart Monday through Thursday most weeks. It just didn't make sense at the time for us to combine our two households while we were both still working. DJ traveled across the United States to meet with his reinsurance clients, and I was the executive officer of Heartland Foundation in St. Joseph. The round trip from his home to my work is 140 miles.

So, when we landed, we parted in the long-term parking lot, driving away in our own vehicles. This parting was more tender and more difficult than any other.

When I got home, I found my bedroom filled with balloons and streamers. A sign read, "Happy, Happy Birthday! You are so loved. Go, Mom." Our children were there for me from the beginning of this uncertain journey. Their small acts of kindness and caring went a long way.

The next day I returned to the office. First thing every Monday morning, the Foundation team would congregate around the kitchen island in the common space for "huddle" time. It was when we talked about Foundation activities coming up that week. We would discuss project planning and timelines, and whatever the important business of the day or week happened to be. Huddle was also a good opportunity to gather the troops and strengthen the closely knit bond we held with one another. I hesitantly disclosed my news to them, and, over the next days and weeks as the news spread, I received an incredible outpouring of compassion from friends and colleagues throughout Heartland Health and Mosaic Life Care.

I had appointments with five doctors during my first week back, and Carol—my executive assistant and my dear friend—reworked my schedule. While DJ was out of town, my friend Karen had volunteered to accompany me to my appointments. Not only did she provide moral support, she became a second set of ears, listening to the specialists' advice on the best course of treatment. In times like these, I'm told, a patient may hear only twenty-five percent of what is said. There is too much information pouring in and too much emotion involved. By having someone accompany you to your appointments, you get a more accurate understanding of all the information provided by your doctors. Doing so can prevent anxious moments as well as help you communicate back to family members.

Every person's course of treatment is different. It depends on a number of factors: the type of tumor, size of the tumor, lymph nodes involvement, location in your breast, mammogram results related to tumor occurring in one or multicentric quadrants, desire for reconstruction, a person's general health, previous history, and other considerations.

My first appointment at the Breast Center was with Dr. Kate, the general surgeon who would be removing the tumors. She explained my options based on my personal medical circumstances. She firmly stated that the cancer was positioned deep inside my breast, making a lumpectomy difficult at best. The doctor described the lumpectomy as a surgical procedure that removes only the tumor and a small margin of tissue surrounding it. However, in my case, she explained this type of surgery would most likely leave me with a permanently, deformed left breast. She elaborated that with a lumpectomy, a series of radiation treatments would be necessary following surgery. Dr. Kate went on to explain it would be difficult and nearly impossible following radiation to do total breast reconstruction at a later date. Listening to her advice, it was becoming clear to me that this alternative might not be the best choice.

Dr. Kate strongly advocated for a mastectomy—preferably a bi-lateral mastectomy—as the optimal choice. This option would require the general surgeon and a reconstructive (plastic) surgeon to team up during the initial operation. She encouraged me to meet with a plastic surgeon and other specialists before making my decision. She emphasized the importance of choosing my treatment path within the week because, while my cancer was not the most aggressive, it was not the slowest growing kind. Also, with the surgery center being heavily booked, getting a date and time placed on the operating room docket could take a couple of weeks. Time was of the essence.

Appointments followed with the radiation oncologist, the medical oncologist, and the nurse navigator from the Breast Center. Finally, I caved and set an appointment with the plastic surgeon—all in the flurry of the first few days from returning home. My head felt like it was spinning.

The radiation oncologist was the third physician to examine my test results and mammography images. This physician specializes in using radiation (x-ray) therapy to treat the local area of the disease and kill any remaining cancer cells in that part of the body.

The radiation oncologist conducted a breast exam and searched for the tumors near my chest wall. I experienced enormous pain as she poked and prodded for what seemed like an eternity. As she was doing this, she explained how radiation therapy works. Most patients will receive daily therapy for six to seven weeks following surgery. She said the treatment goal is to destroy any remaining microscopic cells to prevent further recurrence. Lastly, she covered potential side effects and other matters of concern.

The medical oncologist's office was on the other side of the free-standing Cancer Center, directly across from the radiation oncology offices. A medical oncologist specializes in internal medicine and in the treatment of cancer. The oncologist will determine a treatment plan based on a variety of methods including chemotherapy, immunotherapy, and hormonal therapy.

As I sat with Karen in the waiting room, Tracy, the mother of my son Ryan's friend, came over to say hello. A cancer survivor herself, Tracy worked as a volunteer ambassador at the Cancer Center, and her role was to support women who had recently been diagnosed. She seemed healthy and energetic as a breast cancer survivor, and that gave me hope I could also beat this disease and feel normal again.

I liked Dr. AJ, my medical oncologist, right away. He was compassionate, informative, and he is recognized as an outstanding and highly competent cancer specialist. Unlike the other doctors I saw that week, Dr. AJ said he had all the critical information he needed in the pathology report and a breast exam would not be necessary. What a relief! While looking over my results, he talked about the characteristics of my cancer cells. He referred to the hormone receptor assay test that measures both estrogen and progesterone receptors in the tumor. In my case, the pathology report showed my hormone count was extremely high, meaning the tumors were stimulated to grow by female hormones.

Collecting the pieces of the puzzle, Dr. AJ was tasked with evaluating my situation and designing the best course of post-surgery treatment. But before he made his recommendation, I had a life-changing decision to make. A lumpectomy or a mastectomy?

Stephanie, the nurse navigator, was next. This was the only time that week I went alone.

As I sat in the waiting room, a colleague who was one of Mosaic's marketing specialists walked into the Center. Marcie worked closely with the Breast Center staff and other departments on marketing, promotion, and funding strategies. Knowing she was unaware of my diagnosis, I suddenly felt embarrassed and vulnerable when I saw her. I just wanted to hide. I felt this strange rush of emotions. Perhaps, it's my private nature. One thing was certain: It was all too new and scary to reveal to others. We exchanged a quick, cordial greeting acknowledging one another, and I swiftly looked away.

My name was called moments later, and I was quietly escorted down the hallway into a patient room. As soon as my vitals were taken, Stephanie stepped into the room and introduced herself. She immediately made me feel comfortable. She patiently answered all of my questions, and she let me know the medical team would be there for my cancer journey and for the rest of my life. My initial thought was "let's hope and pray it's a long one."

Before leaving, Stephanie handed me a pink bagful of materials related to the disease and what a patient can expect. One resource was a book called *Breast Cancer Treatment Handbook* by Judy K. Kneece, RN, OCN. The book helps newly diagnosed patients understand the disease, treatments, emotions, and recovery from breast cancer.

As I was about to leave the Breast Center, which was located in the middle of Plaza One, I was suddenly overcome by a feeling of dread. Was it dread? Or was it something else? I don't know, but as I looked at the parking lot, knowing I had to carry that pink bag through the plaza's lobby and all the way to my car, I felt strangely exposed. It was the same feeling I had when I saw Marcie in the waiting room. That same wave of emotions: embarrassment, guilt, sadness, and fear. To this day, I do not understand where the feelings of embarrassment and guilt came from, except from the range of emotions that raged inside me. As one of the senior executive officers on the Heartland Health and Mosaic Life Care team, I knew dozens of people in the clinic building. Many of them I knew quite well. I simply did not want to advertise to anyone that I had cancer. It had been only ten days since I had received the news, and it was still way too fresh. Again, was it my quiet nature? Or was I sensing how my mom felt all those years ago and why her secret was withheld from me for so many years? Whatever the reason, I hurriedly dodged out of the medical center and headed directly to my car in the parking lot as fast as I could, hoping not to run into anyone I knew.

Karen once again accompanied me to my last appointment of the week, the plastic surgeon. Dr. A and I immediately bonded. For my initial visit, Dr. A did a breast exam and took photos of me from the waist up. At this point, so many medical professionals had viewed my bare chest it felt completely normal to pose for nude photographs. I raised my left arm high above my head and then grasped the back of my neck as if posing for a magazine centerfold. It took away the tension as Dr. A; his surgical assistant, Becky; Karen; and I all belly-laughed. I realized at that moment just how important laughter would be to get through the days, months, and what became years ahead.

Dr. A then presented a portfolio of photographs

showing women's chests in the various stages of reconstructive surgery. Women of all shapes and sizes. Clearly, cancer does not come in just one size. The initial photos of those who had just gone through a mastectomy depicting the earliest stage of reconstruction were the most shocking. When I viewed those graphic images, a wave of fear and uncertainty washed over me. I was given a real and raw picture of what I could expect. It was a tough pill to swallow. Then came the after photos of those who completed the total reconstruction process. Even with faintly visible scars, the idea of this approach seemed a bit more bearable. I was beginning to understand reconstruction could help restore your body image following a mastectomy.

Dr. A described the two types of reconstructive surgeries to consider. One necessitates borrowing tissue from your own body, which could be from either your abdomen, your back, or both. The second type involves two surgeries. The first surgery requires placing a temporary tissue expander underneath the pectoral muscle or, in some cases, placing a cadaver skin flap above the muscle. For the next two months, the treatment includes injecting repeatable saline solution fills into the expander implant every week until the desired size is reached. After healing for a few months, the second surgery is scheduled to replace the temporary implants with permanent silicone implants. Any reconstructive surgery, however, would have to wait as much as a year if radiation is required after the mastectomy.

Dr. A thoroughly discussed what was facing me if I

chose a bilateral mastectomy and reconstruction. "It's a long journey," he said, "You become a part of a clinic family and will see one another over long spectrums of your life. Finding a good match of your own communication style with that of your care team is important in developing a healthy and supportive relationship with one another."

I liked Dr. A's philosophy in treating his patients. He said, "When you face hard times, don't think about what the year(s) ahead looks like or even the month. Don't dwell on how many chemo or radiation treatments you have left. Think 'all I have to do is get to the end of this day.' It makes it more manageable and not so overwhelming." He went on to say, "Take comfort in knowing others have been through this very same thing, and they made it out successfully. You'll get past the harder times when you focus on the life that is around you."

While I was considering the best course of treatment, one of my best friends from my college days at the University of Kansas, Cathy, called me. She was one of a few friends who knew about my cancer. She encouraged me to connect with Joyce, an Alpha Chi Omega sorority sister who is now a radiologist. I contacted Joyce immediately, and she asked me to send her all of my test results. She became a valuable resource for a second opinion. Joyce had reached a similar decision point in her life when she opted to have a double mastectomy some years ago. She highly recommended I opt for a double mastectomy with breast reconstruction.

This was not the first time I had received this advice from a friend in the medical field. I had called my physician friend Lindy the day DJ and I drove to Stapleton Airport in Denver. As I shared the news with her, she said, "Judy, you're not going to like what I have to say, but you need to have a double mastectomy." She went on to say, "Too many times I've seen breast cancer come back with a vengeance." And yes, it terrified me to hear those words from Lindy, a dear friend and a medical professional I trust.

Now, after talking to Joyce and weighing Lindy's words, it was becoming more apparent to me that a double mastectomy would reduce the possibility of cancer popping up again or showing up in the other breast. That is what I decided.

Recalling my plastic surgeon's words, "There is no perfect answer. Examine the statistics and facts. You'll never regret getting the information. Then decide what will give you the most peace." He stressed the importance of having "a realistic expectation of how and why we're doing things. More information leads to better patient compliance."

To his point, Stephanie, my nurse navigator, had encouraged me to do genetic testing to see if I carried the gene mutation that raises the risk for breast cancer for family members. The simple test checks for BRCA1 and BRCA2 genetic mutations.

While looking for more information, I found this from the CDC: "About fifty out of 100 women with BRCA1 or BRCA2 will get breast cancer by the time they turn seventy years old compared to seven out of 100 women in the general U.S. population. About thirty out of 100 women with the BRCA mutations will get ovarian cancer by the time they turn seventy compared to one out of 100."

Because my mother was diagnosed with breast cancer, Stephanie believed it was important to find out if I carried one or both of the mutations. Certainly, it was important for my children and grandchildren to know if they were at a higher risk.

Stephanie set up a phone appointment for me to talk with a genetics counselor about the testing, and I spoke with the counselor several times. A simple mouth swab was all it would take from me. I went back to the Breast Center to have it done, thinking I would get the test results back. I soon found out that the analysis of the test was very involved and not cheap.

Unfortunately, the insurance company denied approval of the BRCA1 and BRCA2 testing. The analysis would cost $5,000.

It was denied not just once but four times. Their response for the denials were consistent: I was too old. My oncologist strongly advocated for me each time, and I appealed to the company myself, citing the family history of breast cancer and the need for my children and grandchildren to know if they were a higher risk. After the fourth rejection, the insurance company notified me that only one more appeal would be allowed. My oncologist suggested we contact the physician administrator for Clinical Care and ask for his assistance.

With his agreement to join our battle, our last appeal was finally approved. It pays to fight on.

The test results came back. Fortunately, I did not carry either one of the gene mutations.

Making a decision on the right treatment plan requires much research. It demands open communication with those you are considering for your medical team. It necessitates open conversation with your significant other. Most of all, it requires a lot of soul-searching. So I dived into the research, knowing a decision had to be made soon.

The first full weekend DJ and I were back from California, Jordan made the eight-hour round trip between St. Louis and Kansas City to give me support and to belatedly celebrate my birthday. She and I met at The Classic Cup on The Plaza in KC, and, after hugging for some time, she gave me two presents.

The first one was a beautiful bouquet of mixed flowers including gladiolas, roses, and Gerber daisies. Inside a gift bag was the second present, a book written and illustrated by M.H. Clark called *FIGHT ON!* The author encourages readers to be bold and to be strong. Jordan also handed me a greeting card with a photo enclosed. All of her then co-workers from TEKSystems had taken a group photo—men and women, all wearing pink shirts and tops. People I'd never met but who expressed their love and genuine concern for Jordan and her mother. I was touched.

Following lunch, Jordan and I crossed the street to Barnes and Noble. Our mission was to find thoughtful and reassuring books written about breast cancer. To our dismay, only a few books on the topic were on the shelves, and all but one portrayed the disease with a negative vibe.

I later asked Dr. A what resources he would recommend. One was the American Society for Plastic Surgeons website, which is dedicated to providing good information about breast cancer. He also said, "Rely on your breast cancer medical team, support groups, and online communication. Most importantly, find resources that share a positive view, instead of those that can give a lot of worries that are not valid." He added, "Surround yourself with good information versus bad. Keep moving forward and getting back to a normal life."

Each person has a learning style that works best for them. For me, I chose not to participate in a support group because of my private nature. Instead, I relied on my medical team, my family, my closest friends, and my faith.

It was all beginning to sink in. One week after meeting with all the medical specialists, DJ and I agreed the bilateral mastectomy with the reconstruction option was likely the best choice for my treatment. Choosing to have the two-stage reconstruction meant the need for two major surgeries. The first one required a surgery team including the general surgeon, Dr. Kate, and plastic surgeon, Dr. A, working together. Dr. Kate's role would involve removing both breasts and some of the skin that covered the breast tissue. During the same surgical procedure, Dr. A would then place two temporary tissue expanders under the chest wall.

Following surgery, multiple visits to Dr. A's office would be required to fill both tissue expanders by injecting them with a saline solution. A second surgery then would be performed by Dr. A to replace the temporary expanders with permanent implants filled with liquid silicone gel.

With the decision made, my general surgeon and plastic surgeon coordinated their schedules for a time the two of them could do the lengthy procedure together. The seven-hour surgery was booked for October 17. Little did DJ and I realize the long road that lay ahead of us. The battle was just beginning!

A Pearl of Wisdom:
Live in the Moment

In those first weeks following my diagnosis, questions surrounded me as I grasped my situation and the uncertainty of what was awaiting me. What was my destiny? I felt as if my life were suddenly out of control. I couldn't express what was raging inside of me.

Then, I looked to God and surrendered to Him. He turned my weakness and helplessness into strength. I still had moments of darkness and pain, yet I knew deep in my soul that He was with me, and He placed others in my life to lean on. And boy, did I need those relationships to help lift me up.

Meditate on the healing deep within you. Breathe in the acts of kindness. Find comfort in the challenging times. Live joyfully. Focus on the present. Live in the moment.

Chapter 12

Learning to Dance
in the Rain

As THE DAY OF my surgery approached, DJ and I took advantage of every moment we had together. We talked about everything under the sun. Read spiritually uplifting books together. Listened to music and danced cheek to cheek. Took short, reflective walks on the hiking trail near our home. Most importantly, we prayed and meditated. DJ was still traveling for work, but he and I treasured our weekends together. He was and is my forever love.

The next couple of weeks flew by. At one of my pre-surgery appointments with Dr. A, I jokingly, yet half seriously, asked him if he would tattoo a pink butterfly on my chest as a badge of courage. He said he didn't do that, although he did have a tattoo artist to recommend. Sparing a mastectomy patient's nipples is not always possible. Sometimes the cancer is too close to the nipple, and there is too much skin involved. Sometimes auxiliary nodes are affected. For these patients, a tattoo artist may ink new ones on their breasts after reconstruction and healing. Who would have thought?

Kristen, my son Ryan's wife, gave birth to Natalie Ann on September 30. She was their first child, my first grandchild. The next weekend, DJ and I drove to St. Louis to give me a chance to hold Natalie before my surgery. So precious. I instantly fell in love with her. With all the uncertainty I was facing, it was a gift to cradle hope in my arms. That experience reminded me to grab ahold of each moment.

The weekend before my first surgery, Karen, her husband Mark, and another friend, Martha, met DJ and me for dinner and drinks at La Bodega's Spanish Tapas Restaurant at 119th Street in Lenexa, Kansas. Friends are priceless. We laughed heartily and embraced our deep, decades-long friendship that night. They gave me cards and presents. One of the presents from Karen was a crystal pink butterfly, a symbol of this transitioning and transformative time as my new life was unfolding. Another from Martha was a Build-A-Bear monkey with aviator sunglasses and a heroic Superman cape and outfit, signifying a readiness to fight on. Martha said patients going through a mastectomy are encouraged to take a stuffed animal with them to the hospital to have something soft and snuggly to hold.

Our server asked what the big celebration was all about, and I said, making a joke, "I'm getting new breasts on Thursday."

"Wow! That sounds cool!" he said, and he obviously thought I was having breast enlargement surgery. I told him I was having a double mastectomy and reconstruction surgery. It put him in an awkward position, and he stumbled for something to say. "My aunt had breast cancer," he said. "She died."

It was just what I didn't need to hear, but the waiter's statement made me deeply aware that not everyone survives this journey.

Here's the harsh reality, according to the National Breast Cancer Foundation. Breast cancer is:

- The most commonly diagnosed cancer in women;
- The second leading cause of cancer death among women;
- Is diagnosed in over 250,000 women in the United States each year with more than 40,000 dying annually. So, one in six die. Stated differently, one woman succumbs to breast cancer every thirteen minutes.

A few days before my surgery, Karen joined me on a shopping trip to buy appropriate clothes to wear during the recovery process. We shopped at TJ Maxx and Target for loose-fitting, comfortable tops and sweat pants. I found both Ninja Turtle warrior and army camo sweats that were a must for my new wardrobe. Quite the change from a career woman's attire.

The people I worked with at the Foundation were immeasurably supportive. On the last day at work before my medical leave, they showered me with gifts—crossword puzzles, Sudoku games, lollipops and chocolates, a warm fluffy blanket, an overnight bag, and sharpened pencils. They also presented me with a silver bracelet with different charms, including a cross, an amulet with the inscription FAITH, a red dress symbolizing my wedding dress, and a pink ribbon standing for the fight against breast cancer. Each one of the Foundation team members also had the same bracelet and pledged to wear it through my surgery and recovery. Two additional bracelets were made. One was for Jordan and one for Karen.

Then, on Wednesday, October 16, my medical leave began, so I could prep emotionally before being admitted to the hospital early the next morning. Connecting with nature has always been important to me. I decided to go on a leisurely walk early that morning and take in the sights around me. Then it hit me. What if I didn't wake up from the anesthetic? Was it possible this might be my last full day on earth? Recalling past surgeries that lasted only a couple of hours, it was always difficult for me to wake up. And I was going under for a seven-hour procedure?

I paid attention to every detail around me that morning. The birds chirping, the warmth of the October sun, the gentle breeze across my face, the colorful fall foliage, and the fragrance of fresh air. This planet really is a beautiful place. We can easily miss it if we do not take the time to notice its striking beauty.

Jordan drove in from St. Louis, and we went to the East Hills Mall to pick out some additional post-surgical clothing. At Victoria Secret's PINK Store, we found a light gray jacket with sparkling rhinestones outlining the shape of angel wings on the back side. It was the perfect jacket to wear to and from the hospital for my surgeries. We looked for hope in the smallest things, because it was such a scary time for all of us. Although it was just a jacket with angel wings, it was a symbol representing strength, hope, faith, and courage.

DJ arrived late in the afternoon. The three of us had a quiet evening at home, enjoying grab-and-go meals from Ground Round. We made sure our time together was as normal as possible.

Our hearts were filled with gratitude from the outpouring of support and prayers from family members, friends, my in-laws, co-workers, people from Ashland United Methodist Church, and a number of prayer circles. And yes, even strangers, including an unknown quilting group who sent me a prayer quilt with blocks of different patterned fabrics and biblical scriptures. Carol, my executive assistant, told me her brother, who was living in Asia, had requested that the monks from a Buddhist monastery there offer prayers for my healing.

DJ, Jordan, and I arrived at the hospital at 5:30 Thursday morning, October 17. Karen met us at the pre-op room an hour or so later. Shortly after she arrived, a medical transporter whisked me away to another room. A radiology professional introduced himself as he explained the mapping procedure he was about to perform; it was a necessary step before my surgery. Sentinel lymph node mapping is a test that determines whether the cancer has spread or metastasized to the lymph nodes area. It starts with an injection of a radioactive substance shot into your breast before you go to the operating room. In my case, the surgeon ordered an injection in both breasts. The precautionary step was done in case cancer was detected in the other breast.

The radiology technician first applied a bit of lidocaine to my left breast in an attempt to numb the area. Unfortunately, after inserting the long needle in my breast I felt excruciating pain. I felt like screaming. The lidocaine only numbed the surface of my skin. Did I really have to go through this procedure on my other side, too? Then, he applied the lidocaine on the other breast. As I held my breath, he injected my right side with the radioactive substance. Finally, the procedure was over. The medical transporter arrived and wheeled me on the gurney back to the pre-op room. DJ, Jordan, and Karen (aka The Pink Brigade) were there. We quietly waited together.

Soon after, one of the nurse anesthetists came by to insert an IV in preparation for my surgery. She placed the needle into my right hand between the thumb and forefinger to seek a vein but missed and hit a nerve.

Not knowing what she did, the anesthetist continued to push the needle in further to the nerve causing stinging, unbearable pain. I let out a scream when she suddenly realized what had just happened and rapidly withdrew the needle. She then left to find someone else to insert the IV. For the next five years, I would experience numbness in that part of my hand. Needless, to say, it was a rough start, especially knowing the most traumatic part was still ahead.

Then, Dr. Kay, my primary anesthesiologist, arrived and inserted the IV in the crease of my left arm in preparation for my operation. Knowing what had just happened, she injected a small amount of anesthetic cocktail through the IV to calm my nerves and numb the pain in my hand. The light sedative warmly flowed throughout my body.

Sally and, a bit later, another chaplain friend came by to offer prayers. And, boy, were prayers needed at that time. I instantly felt a sense of peace and comfort.

All of my other doctors followed Dr. Kay and came by to see me: the general surgeon, the plastic surgeon, and even my primary care doctor. They gave last-minute directives and answered any questions we had. The surgeon strategically used a black marking pen to outline where the incisions would be made on my body to surgically remove my breasts.

Then, it was time. Dr. Kay gave another small dose of anesthetic intravenously in the sedation process. The Pink Brigade, which now included Lindy, offered loving thoughts as I found myself slipping away into the fog. I remember being placed on a gurney and wheeling into the hallway. And then I was out like a light.

Years later, Lindy would share with me what was happening in the surgical waiting room while I was on the operating table. They all knew a long day was ahead of them. Jordan settled in on the other side of the room doing work on the computer out of her office, while Karen, Lindy, and DJ were seated together. Shortly after they started the waiting period, DJ slumped down in his chair and tears began to roll down his cheeks. He told Karen and Lindy, "I can't live without Judy. I can't lose her to cancer." He had already lost his first wife, Pam, to cancer. Lindy described how his "pent up emotion seemed to come out."

"It's like many husbands and family members who had kept up the good fight," she said. "But the emotion and stress catch up." She said that it was like, "DJ felt every cut of the scalpel, every stitch that was made, and he felt helpless. There was nothing he could do but rely on the medical professionals who were there to take care of his wife."

Karen and Lindy reassured him I was in good hands. They switched the conversation to the healing phase. The two friends said they would make certain I would not be alone or treated any differently because of this disease. My Pink Brigade was definitely in it for the long haul. The surgery took just over seven hours before I was moved to the surgical recovery room.

The next thing I knew, I was waking up and coming out of the anesthesia in my hospital room. Still in a foggy state, it felt like a mother elephant was sitting on my chest. Uncomfortable does not even begin to describe the pain I experienced that day. Giving birth to three children was a piece of cake compared to this.

DJ and Jordan stayed with me at the hospital the next few days and, of course, at our home in St. Joseph for the first week. Despite my being heavily medicated, my compassionate nurse mates would insist on getting me up to walk the halls of the hospital wing post-surgery. It was definitely time to move forward in this battle.

As I lay in the hospital bed, the magic cocktail of intravenous pain medications made me groggy, but it helped to somewhat dull the throbbing pain. My arms felt limp. I needed help to put a robe on. I noticed two eighteen-inch drainage tubes hanging from my sides. There was a plastic bulb attached to the end of each tube to collect blood and fluids from my chest area. The tubes were securely stitched inside my chest. Every hour or so the nurses emptied the bulbs while measuring the accumulated fluids.

After a rough few days and nights in the hospital, I was sent home. The Pink Brigade became my "home health" nurse mates and took on many tasks, including the job of emptying the blood contents from the drainage tube bulbs. I was simply too weak to do so. In fact, it was weeks before I could lift my arms to dress myself or even wash my hair.

Karen took on the role of care manager and kept family, friends, and colleagues informed. I wasn't ready to see anyone outside a small tight circle of just a few loved ones. Even while I was in the hospital, she curtailed visitors. Getting uninterrupted time to rest allowed me to focus on both the physical and emotional healing that was essential to my recovery.

The pathology report came back following my surgery. The results identified a new carcinoma that was growing in the right breast tissue, my supposedly good breast. Thank goodness I decided to have a double mastectomy. The brighter news from the mapping test indicated no cancer cells growing in my lymph nodes. Thankfully, chemotherapy would not be necessary.

Once released from the hospital, I stayed at the house in St. Joseph to be near my surgeons should complications arise. When DJ and Jordan headed back to work, Karen arranged "sitters" to stay at scheduled times for those days and overnights when Karen or Lindy could not stay.

As soon as my surgeon gave the green light, I finished my last few weeks of medical leave recovering at our home in Overland Park. DJ delayed his out-of-town travel schedule and worked from home during that time.

I remember watching endless hours of television, mainly comedies like *Modern Family* and *The Office.* Even though it hurt to laugh, it also was a huge relief. It made me feel more normal in what were abnormal circumstances. For the first few weeks, I slept while sitting up in an easy chair with an ottoman to prop my legs and feet off the floor. Lying on my back proved to be way too uncomfortable. Reading was out because my vision was blurred more than usual from the after-effects of the anesthesia. Even wearing my glasses did not help. DJ would oftentimes read to me before turning out the lights for the night.

My friend Carol R. was one of my trusted sitters. Along with a book—*The Silver Lining* by Hollye Jacobs, RN—about the author's own breast cancer journey, Carol gave me a card I still cherish to this day. It reads: *Don't wait for the storms to pass! Learn to dance in the rain.* How very profound those words were, and are, as they still resonate with me today.

Dr. A would see me every week to continue the two-stage reconstruction process. He would inject a small amount of saline solution into each implant to expand my skin and chest wall. As my temporary implants, otherwise known as "the girls," were filled over time, it felt as if I were carrying heavy rocks in my chest.

The first phase of the reconstruction process was moving along successfully and had started to restore my body image. Now I needed to wait several months and then go in for my second procedure to remove the temporary implants and replace them with new permanent silicone implants. The primary advantage to choosing silicone over saline implants as my per-manent "girls" is the thick silicone gel-filled implants feel more natural. For now, though, I just needed more healing time before undergoing a second operation so this replacement could happen.

Four weeks had passed since the first surgery, and I

was now ready to return to work. The Saturday before, DJ and I decided to see a movie at AMC Theatres. It would be my first outing. I showered and noticed that my right breast was red and hot to touch. Dr. A said if there were any sign of infection to call immediately. Not wanting to overreact, we decided to go to the movie that afternoon and would check to see if there had been any change once we were back home. After all, my next appointment with the plastic surgeon was less than two days away.

When we returned home from the movie, my chest was still bright red and hot to touch. DJ and I talked about whether I should call the doctor on a Saturday or just wait until I saw him Monday afternoon for the scheduled appointment. I felt just fine. Going back and forth on what to do, we were leaning towards waiting until Monday. Then, as if nudged, I remembered that Dr. A said to call if there was *any* noticeable sign of a possible infection. It was time to call.

I contacted Mosaic's nurse hotline and told the attending nurse my name, about the recent surgery for breast cancer and now this sudden redness and heat. I also mentioned that my next appointment with Dr. A was on Monday and wondered if I should just wait to see the doctor at that time.

The nurse identified herself as Avis, a colleague and friend of mine. Without delay, she made a call to connect with the on-call physician that weekend. I was immediately started on two, high-powered oral antibiotics and told to follow up with Dr. A on Monday. Her closing words were jarring when she stated, "Judy, I'm glad you got me. I may have just saved your life."

Lindy later shared her thoughts about calling the nurse hotline that day. She said if I had waited until my doctor's appointment just two days later, it very well could have been too late. Lindy went on to explain, "When an overwhelming bacterial infection starts, it can get into your blood stream causing sepsis; it's oftentimes difficult to get ahead of and can be life threatening." No doubt God and my guardian angels were watching over me.

DJ flew out on Monday morning for work, while Karen accompanied me to the doctor's office. Upon baring my chest, I could tell Dr. A was concerned. Even with the two high-powered antibiotics in my system, the redness and heat were still present. Using a needle syringe, he took a fluid sample from my breast area and sent it off to test for any bacterial infection. He was ada-mant I not eat or drink anything in case we had to go in for emergency surgery that night. A few hours later, he called me to say that nothing had been determined, but they wanted the culture to grow overnight to see if anything changed.

The next day the doctor called with the grim news. Yes, the lab specimen tested positive for a bacterial infection. Surgery would be necessary. In addition to the two oral antibiotics I was taking, I went to the hospital for IV antibiotics the next two days prior to surgery on Thursday. DJ rearranged his schedule, flew back home, and arrived at the hospital just as I was going into surgery.

Dr. A determined it was imperative to remove the temporary breast implant on my right side. Besides cleaning my chest out from all the infection, he would need to remove and dispose the implant expander. After I asked if he would insert a new device during surgery, he advised against it, stating, "You don't realize how dangerous this is." He wanted to make sure the bacterial infection was gone—completely gone. Even if a new sterile temporary implant was put in, foreign devices in the body are like a magnet that easily attract bacterial microbes. That meant waiting six months to ensure I was infection-free and completely healed before surgically implanting a new temporary implant and starting the reconstruction process all over again.

After my second surgery and a post-op visit, the doctor told me that in a couple of days I may remove my bandages at home. I stood in front of the bathroom mirror while Jordan carefully unfurled the bindings from my chest. She cautiously avoided the new drainage device that was securely stitched inside my chest with its elongated tube and bulb dangling at my side.

Seeing my reflection in the mirror, I was shocked to see my chest on the right side was hollow and concave. I felt light-headed and nearly fainted. My face was ashen. I quickly sat down on the cold bathroom floor to catch my breath and instantly knew how my mother must have felt. Shocked and saddened, I did not want my new husband to see me this way. With Jordan standing there, I instantly broke down and cried. DJ was soon to arrive at our St. Joseph house that afternoon.

The minute DJ walked through the front door, we hugged and I buried my face deep in his chest and sobbed. Now sixty-one years old, I had waited thirteen years after my divorce to find DJ. Only three months after our wedding day I was diagnosed with cancer and now this. I wondered what effect this delay would have on successfully completing reconstruction and how would it impact my relationship with my husband. Would he still find me attractive? At least another two major surgeries awaited us. We had been through so much together already in the five short months we had been married.

Now as he held me at the front door, he gently assured me once again, "We will get through this together."

A Pearl of Wisdom:

Embrace an Attitude of Gratitude

DJ recently said, "Even in our deepest darkest valleys, we find ways to celebrate life."

That's so true. His thought ties back to something our friend Deena once shared, "It's all about having an attitude of gratitude."

Everyone faces storms in their life. A serious illness, a broken heart, the loss of a loved one, or some other adversity in one's labyrinth of existence. When those times occur, be open to embracing head-on what may be a life-changing moment. Those dark periods may just open your heart and soul to new ways of thinking, creating, doing, and living. By changing your mindset from one of anger, sadness, and/or fear to an attitude of gratitude, you will reap abundant blessings. I learned when you shift your day-to-day focus to the blessings and world that surround you, you will get through the difficult times. Embrace those times with an attitude of gratitude!

Chapter 13

Miracles Do Happen

"TRY TO GET BACK to a normal life as soon as possible." That's what my surgeon, Dr. A, told me. "Go back to your regular regimen because focusing on life instead of the disease helps us get beyond the tougher times quicker."

I took that advice to heart, and on January 5, some eleven weeks after the double mastectomy, I returned to work. More surgery awaited me, but for now I needed my normal life back. And that meant keeping our plans to return to Sedona, our sacred place, in mid-February.

My recovery was going as well as expected, but I knew I wouldn't be able to enjoy all of the strenuous outdoor activities DJ and I were accustomed to. Strangely, it wasn't the cancer surgeries that held me down. It was the back injury I had suffered almost ten months earlier.

Just a couple of months before our wedding, I had slipped on the freshly waxed wooden stairs. My feet went out from under me and my lower back sharply hit the edge of the last stair. I couldn't move. The pain was intense. I was terrified I had broken something. I lay sprawled out on my back on the floor for ten minutes. Ever so carefully, I rolled over and pushed myself up on my hands and knees. Bracing myself and grabbing the corner of the wall between the dining room and kitchen, I gradually stood up.

Somehow, I managed to make it to work that day, even though the pain was so intense that it ran from the middle of my lower back all the way down my left leg. I called the doctor and had x-rays that day. The diagnosis: a bulging disc, stenosis, and a pinched nerve running down my left leg. I was referred to the local pain clinic, where I opted for cortisone shots and physical therapy over potentially addictive pain medications. No matter which option I chose, however, my active life was suddenly curtailed. I am a longtime runner, kickboxer, cardio exerciser, snow skier, avid hiker, and strength trainee, and now any fitness activities had to be placed on hold.

Shortly after the fall, I saw my primary care physician for an annual wellness check. My doctor knew my lifestyle. In fact, at one point, my doctor and I participated in the same kickboxing classes. She looked at my medical record, saw the scans of my lower spine, and read the diagnosis. She said quite simply, "Judy, your days of doing rigorous cardio exercise are over." Ugh!

Prior to the back injury, DJ and I would go on five-mile walks on the hiking trails in Overland Park most weekends. After the fall, we continued to walk. Only now I found myself limping and experiencing severe pain after less than half a mile. Pain raged from the lower section of my spine all the way down my leg to the top of my ankle. Needless to say, I was finished.

At times I would have to pick up my left leg under the kneecap to get into a car. Climbing stairs meant leading with my right foot for every step up the staircase. I simply lacked the strength in my left leg to walk up a set of stairs in a normal fashion.

Cortisone shots and physical therapy provided some relief, but it was clear this would be a chronic medical condition. As far as I was concerned, surgery was a risk with no guarantee and pain meds could offer only a temporary fix for an issue that wasn't going away.

Sedona has always been a magical place for us. It is where the birds flocked around us and angels seemed to gather, where DJ proposed to me, and where we got married. When we returned in February 2015, I was hobbled by back issues and I was still in the midst of cancer recovery, but the place was just as wondrous.

On our second day back in Sedona, we ran into an acquaintance we had met on our first visit. Knowing our love for hiking and learning of my back issue, she suggested we meet with a friend of hers named Deena Lee. Deena is a medical intuitive and healer. Looking at each other, DJ and I both thought, "What do we have to lose?"

DJ, our friend, and I trekked over to Deena's office just a short distance away. We knew there was only a small chance she would be able to get me in for an appointment during our brief time in Arizona, let alone see us that day.

Our friend introduced us to Deena, a sixty-something petite woman with a broad smile, and told her why we came to see her. Amazingly, Deena told us that her eleven o'clock appointment had car problems and had just canceled.

"If you'd like, I can see you now," Deena said, and then, just as surprisingly, she added, "We've met before."

Slightly puzzled by her comment, DJ and I assured her that was not the case. Perhaps she noticed us when we visited with our friend on our last visit to Sedona. She said with assurance, "I'm sure I've met you before."

After a bit of small talk, she escorted DJ and me back to the clinical treatment room. She asked me to take off my shoes and lie face down on the patient table. I mentioned to Deena I had had two recent surgeries.

"I know," she said, "and your cancer is gone." Her words sent chills up my spine. How could she possibly know I had cancer?

In addition to the treatment table, the room had a large aquarium with brightly colored tropical fish, an oil painting of an eagle soaring in the sky, and soft meditative music in the background. A small rectangular table against the back wall had a set of five battery-operated candles sitting on top. All but one of the candles were brightly shining. DJ told me later, when we were comparing notes, that he had noticed the bulb was lying on the table, next to the candle that was not working.

Face down on the table, I felt Deena gently place her hands on my shoulders and gradually move them down my spine. I noticed how incredibly hot her hands were. DJ stood beside the treatment table and watched as she applied her healing touch, all the way down my left leg and ankle. She placed my feet together and said, "Your legs are uneven. One leg seems to be visibly shorter than the other." I lay completely still with my eyes closed tightly as she continued her therapeutic care.

While she was holding my feet together, I heard Deena say as if surprised, "Did you see that?"

DJ, with an expression of wonder and awe in his voice said, "Yes, I did!"

Because my eyes were closed, I had no idea what they were talking about. DJ explained what he had witnessed. The candle with the missing bulb magically flashed and flickered for a number of seconds before going out.

"There's no bulb in that candle. How did that happen?" my husband remarked. He even walked over to the table to make sure. No evidence of a bulb or light source was found. How could that be?

Deena promptly said, "A miracle is taking place here today." She continued to gently press, or should

I say touch, my lower back. She then checked my feet again, which were now perfectly aligned side by side. She had me lie quietly for about ten minutes, then asked me to sit up and take my time getting down from the treatment table.

After I put my shoes on, she instructed me to walk down the narrow hallway and back to the treatment room. As I did so, Deena stated, "You're even walking taller than when you came here."

I noticed there was not an ounce of pain in my body. None. Prior to this visit and for nearly one year, I had experienced chronic and at times excruciating pain each and every day. Now, I was pain free.

She advised me to drink plenty of water the rest of the day and when I felt the need to sleep, "Do so until you wake up on your own." She also reinforced to my husband that it was important for my body to rest and not to wake me when I fell asleep.

Deena encouraged me to go hiking that day. Following lunch, we did just that. In fact, we drove to nearby Flagstaff and walked all over that quaint town for more than two hours. Returning to Sedona mid-afternoon, we even hiked up to the Summit on Airport Loop to meditate and take in the beautiful surroundings of the Red Rocks. Before we left, we hiked the Loop all the way to the spot where DJ proposed to me one year earlier. After nearly a half a day of hiking more than five miles, I had no pain. Just earlier that day, I had struggled to get out of bed.

Our now seven-foot juniper tree near the Airport

Loop Trail was still standing tall. I walked up to it, silently thanking God and my angels. Then I placed two fingers to my lips and gently touched the tree.

As I stepped back, I was stunned to discover our tree wasn't a single tree at all. It was two identical trees joined by one root system. A "soul twin" tree!

Since that day, DJ and I now walk five to seven miles most days of the week. The pain is gone, and only on rare occasions when I've done too much do I experience a bit of discomfort. After all, I am sixty-eight years old.

I realize this all sounds crazy. I don't understand it myself. I can't begin to explain it. I just know a God moment took place that day in February. Why me? I'm not sure, but I'm eternally grateful for the healing.

As DJ and I left Deena's office that day, she shared that she remembered where she had met us. She said, "You came to me in my dream last night."

Believe it or not, miracles do happen.

A Pearl of Wisdom:
Believing Is Seeing

Conventional thinking tells us that we must see something to believe in it. Over the years, I've challenged this myopic reasoning. I've come to understand that if you truly believe, you will see. God gives us a way to do what we couldn't do on our own if we believe. He gives us the strength and dares us to move forward in faith, love, and hope in co-creating a vision and turning it into reality. The Bible verse 2 Corinthians 5:7 proclaims, "We live by faith, not by sight."

No matter how great the challenge in our lives, trust that God will help you make it through. This wisdom can help you through difficulties in your life or to have the confidence to see a visionary plan through to its completion. Believe it, then you will see it!

Chapter 14

A Coincidence?

W<small>E ALL EXPERIENCE MOMENTS</small> in our lives when things just come together. Carl Jung, in *Synchronicity: An Acausal Connecting Principle,* explains this concept as "a meaningful coincidence of two or more events where something other than the probability of chance is involved." Something like that happened to DJ and me in Sedona in 2020.

This was our ninth visit to this magical land, and we had rented a cozy little studio for the entire month of March. We had all that time and didn't want to waste a minute of it. Though, we did sleep in that first morning.

After breakfast, an unexpected downpour forced us to juggle our plans for a hike. Instead, we headed to Uptown Sedona, a tourist mecca, where we knew the storefront overhangs (and our malfunctioning umbrella) would help fend off the rain.

Uptown features a dozen or so tourist depots where sales people pitched their excursions, whatever they might be. There was a train ride through the Verde Canyon, a helicopter flight over the massive Red Rocks formations, hot air balloon rides, and open-air Jeep tours across the awe-inspiring landscape. There were intuitive guides to take tourists out on the hiking trails to experience the mysterious vortex. On our first trips to Sedona, we would stop to chat with some of the sales people to soak up their knowledge, and then we'd sign up for the best deals for some of these exciting adventures. Now we knew the area fairly well, and we were not so easily enticed.

As we walked by one of these adventure-deal kiosks, one young man's sales pitch caught our attention. He had a vibrant personality and a certain magnetism, so we stopped and listened to his entertaining spiel. He welcomed us to Sedona and said, "My name is Taylor."

This pleasant guy asked all sorts of questions about us—who we were, where we were from, what led us to Sedona, and so on. This was routine at these places. The salespeople get personal and try to reel you in. It's effective with a lot of tourists but not so much with us anymore. So after politely answering his questions and giving him a brief version of our story, we turned the tables and asked about him.

Taylor was a longtime resident, he said. His parents still live in Sedona, and his mother is an artist and a teacher. I asked about his mother's work, and Taylor told us her work was featured at The Vue in Tlaquepaque Square. Tlaquepaque Square—or T-Square, as we called it—is an arts and crafts village in the city, and we knew it quite well. Yet I didn't recall a place called The Vue.

I told Taylor we had purchased a painting and a wind sculpture from one of the Rene Taylor galleries there, and, for a brief moment, I wondered if the art piece we had—*Sedona at Dusk* —was one of his mother's works. Not likely. We bought that piece from the featured artist at Rene Taylor's, not The Vue. I did notice his nametag said Taylor Sitts, and I was fairly certain our artist's last name was Sitts.

I asked if his mother displayed her work at the Rene Taylor Gallery, and he said he was certain it was The Vue. He didn't seem to know about the Taylor gallery and its location in T-Square.

We talked with Taylor for twenty minutes or so. These were tough times for a lot of business people in Sedona. With the COVID-19 pandemic rapidly unfolding, there had been a lot of cancellations. Tours were dropped, trips were terminated. This was Spring Break, and it was normally one of the high seasons for tourists. Taylor explained how his trade had been affected and, being the skilled communicator that he is, he made a pitch for a "just recently" offered archaeology tour by the Safari Jeep Company.

The excursion, which he billed as "mysterious and sacred," actually sounded interesting. An off-road Jeep ride would take us into a gated area not available to the public. The expedition also entailed a two-mile hike into the secluded and sprawling terrain to the archaeological site. The site dates back about 1,500 years. It contained the remnants of pit dwellings, petroglyphs etched in igneous rocks, and shards of pottery just lying on the ground. Taylor is very good at what he does, and we signed up for an archaeology Jeep tour during the following week. Before we left him, he also recommended several hiking trails, most of which were previously unknown to us.

A few days later, DJ and I decided to explore T-Square. We walked through the outdoor mall, checking out a few of the eclectic shops, passed dozens of metal wind sculptures whirling in the air, and arrived at our favorite art gallery. That's when I noticed the signboard in front of the gallery. "Rene Taylor's" it read in large letters. And above it was the words: The Vue.

Neither DJ nor I had ever noticed the words "The Vue" before. Apparently, the locals call it that. Inside, Jan Sitts' distinctive artwork was featured prominently. It was obvious now to both of us that Jan Sitts was Taylor's mother.

The next day, we took one of Taylor's hiking recommendations and traveled ten miles north to tackle what was described as an exhilarating nature walk at West Fork. This nature walk is considered the most romantic trail in the Sedona area. Grand cliffs reflect their beauty along this three-and-a-half-mile trail that crossed the gentle Oak Creek in more than a dozen places, forcing hikers to balance as they traversed logs and skipped from stone to stone.

After our hike, we headed back to town and stopped at Uptown in hopes of finding Taylor. We wanted to tell him about the hike to West Fork and to share our discovery about his mother. Taylor wasn't at the kiosk, but the young woman who was working there told us he was at another store for the day. It was a few blocks away, and she offered to take us there. This is one of the reasons we love Sedona so much. People are so open and willing to help perfect strangers.

We found Taylor sitting on a stool behind a counter chatting with another couple. We waited outside, and, when he was free, he joined us with a broad smile. I excitedly shared with him that we have one of his mother's paintings.

"You mean you just bought one of her pieces?"

"No," DJ said, "We purchased the piece over five and a half years ago."

Then we told him the story, how just after our wedding we went to the T-Square, and we were both drawn to this extraordinary abstract painting at Rene Taylor's gallery. It was a piece called *Sedona at Dusk*. Our wedding just happened to be at dusk.

We told Taylor his mother's painting captured everything we felt during that sacred moment on our wedding day. Our angels were with us. The first time we saw the painting, we both noticed what appeared to be an angel watching over us. I also told Taylor that my encore career and avocation is writing, and the title of one of the chapters in my book is called "Sedona at Dusk." The painting now represents even so much more.

Taylor's expression was one of awe, wonder, and emotion. We suddenly felt connected to one another and exchanged phone numbers. Before leaving, a passerby took a photo of the three of us on DJ's iPhone.

I don't know if meeting the son of Jan Sitts qualifies as one of Jung's synchronicities. But Jan's *Sedona at Dusk* is very special to us, and because we met Taylor Sitts as we did, I believe it really was a "meaningful coincidence" where "something other than the probability of chance" was involved.

We returned to Sedona for a month-long stay in February 2021. As soon as we finished unpacking, DJ and I walked to Uptown. As we walked by the kiosk where Taylor worked last year, we were pleasantly surprised to see him again. We chatted for quite a while when he offered to take DJ and me hiking on his day off.

Taylor then asked if we would like to meet his mother and father. For a number of years, we had been just missing Jan at the Rene Taylor Gallery. Now we might finally get a chance to meet the artist and tell her our story behind her artwork, *Sedona at Dusk.*

A few days later, Taylor let us know that his parents had invited us to come by their home for a visit and to see Jan's studio. Ten days later, we shared a glass of wine and shared stories with each other in their home. In addition to creating artwork, Jan teaches her technique to others around the world. We discovered Jan and her husband both grew up in Kansas, and she studied at the Kansas City Art Institute.

As I told Jan our story about DJ proposing to me in Sedona and "That's the Angel" story, she said Robin Anderson from Jerome, Arizona, is a friend of hers. She taught one of her art classes in his gallery. We also talked about our connection to her painting and the special meaning it holds for us. Jan smiled and said, "I think that's what they call synchronicity."

And then Jan and Dick invited us to have dinner with them the next time we come back to Sedona.

Two days later, Taylor picked us up in his Toyota Tacoma for a four-wheeling adventure. He drove us to an area outside of Sedona for a rocky, off-road excursion. After riding about thirty minutes or so, we parked and hiked to a secluded area where no trails existed. We walked and climbed the rugged area. Not another soul in sight. This was definitely back country.

Taylor said the hidden canyon cannot be found on area maps, and only the archaeology club and a few locals know about the place. After climbing up a sharp incline through the native habitat, we made it to the site. There, high in the canyon, was a shelter made by the Sinagua people. The structure dates back to around AD 600. I could feel a chill in the air as we quietly entered the sacred grounds. It was certainly a spiritual experience!

Next, we made our way down an unpaved backroad to Vultee Arch in Lost Canyon. Near the top of the Arch, we could see a panoramic view of the cliffs, geological formations, and red rock terrain. It was stunning. The six-and-a-half-hour trek passed much too quickly.

On our last day, we traveled to Jerome to reconnect with Robin Anderson at his Old Mingus Art Center. His personal studio in the art center was just as we remembered. More than a hundred etchings were displayed on the classroom wall. This time Robin gave us a personal tour of his contemporary artwork collection displayed on the lower floor.

It was a blessing to meet these people. What a bonding moment with each one! Too often we close ourselves off, but when we are open to meeting someone new, there is oftentimes a special connection. Then again, it all happened in Sedona, which has always been a magical and mystical place for us.

A Pearl of Wisdom:

Tune In

Tune in to what's going on in the world around you. In my previous book, *Come Together, Think Ahead*, I describe the concept of coincidence, which has also been called synchronicity. You may experience unexpected incidents in your life. Happenings you never could have imagined. I find these times tend to show up out of nowhere, but these occurrences respond to our intentions.

Joseph Jaworski, in his book *Synchronicity: The Inner Path of Leadership,* describes it as a natural unfolding in which an event that could have never been predicted seems to guide us along our journey.

My life coach, Lee Kaiser, described synchronicity as a "vibrational relationship." He taught that "people … seemingly appear from nowhere to respond, and connect with, our intentions. It is a flood of connections that allows highly intentional people to create in big ways."

I believe these connections are not just a fluke or an accident. They are a phenomenon, a wonder, or perhaps even a miracle.

Einstein has an interesting way of defining this concept. His view of coincidence "is God's way of remaining anonymous." I like this description the best. Because I believe God is ever present in our lives as He and His angels quietly watch over and guide us.

Be open and TUNE IN.

Chapter 15

What?! No Roma?!

ALMOST TEN WEEKS FOLLOWING my third surgery for breast cancer, we were on our way with our dearest friends, Karen and Mark, for a ten-day vacation to Italy. The first part of our journey took us to the Tuscany region, where we stayed in a country villa, an old two-story stone barn that had been converted into guest accommodations. Located in the rambling hills, the villa was isolated with no other residences nearby. The scenic landscape simply took our breath away.

With our rental car, we spent the next five nights and six days exploring the countryside and medieval towns with majestic churches and castles perched on top of cliffs. Each day we would trek across the terrain and pass dozens of vineyards and vast fields of sunflowers in full bloom. On our visits to small villages like Montepulciano, Montalcino, and Siena, we would learn about the local history and do "liquid gold" tastings of Brunello, Noble, and Chianti red wines. Brunello wines were definitely our favorite.

We traveled next to Pisa to see the Leaning Tower, and then we were off to Cinque Terre—which is part of the Italian Riviera. Each of these five exceptional and colorful villages is unique and has its own dialect and proud heritage. No roads reach these villages. They are connected only by a hiking trail, by a commuter train, and by boat. We chose to hop from village to village by water. The twenty-four-hour tour was a whirlwind of activity as the four of us spent one night at the Hotel La Villa degli Argenteri in Monterosso al Mare.

That is where DJ and I said goodbye to Karen and Mark. We were heading to Rome, and they were off to another destination. They are a well-traveled couple, and, before we parted, they advised us about Italian trains, which we would take to Rome. First-class seating, they said, is typically found in the car directly behind the locomotive. Trains usually run late, so don't be surprised by any lack of punctuality.

They also advised us to jump on the train as soon as it arrives because the doors close in a matter of minutes. They told us about how their friends Jennifer and Rob had once boarded a train while traveling in Europe, and, finding no conductor, Rob hopped off to locate one. Then the doors closed, and he was left standing at the depot.

That reminded me of the time I had traveled to Paris and London with Karen and our friend Tamra. On the second night in London, we went to the West End's Theatre District to see *Les Miserables*. We caught the last performance of the day and had to scramble to make it to the train station just before midnight. The platform was crowded with theatergoers making their way home. People were shoulder to shoulder, and as the doors opened it became a rush with everyone shoving and squeezing their way onto the train. Karen and I jumped on, the doors slammed shut, and we looked around for Tamra. There she was, still on the platform, waving goodbye to us as the train pulled away.

With those cautionary tales fresh in our minds, we would be sure not to make any of those mistakes.

We had just three short days and two nights left, and Rome was to be our last stop before heading back home. We boarded a commuter train, and it took us to La Spezia, where we were to catch the bullet train for Rome. Weary from all the travel, we were pleased our travel agent had arranged first-class tickets for this nearly four-hour train ride. With only a light lunch at noon, DJ and I were famished, and we looked forward to our first-class meal and a glass of vino. We had long imagined the opportunity to explore the magnificent sights of Rome, and it was now a dream that was about to come true.

We arrived at the La Spezia station and had no idea which direction the train would be coming from, so I asked an Italian man who was passing by. He cordially told us to wait at the end of Platform Five for the night train. There we joined about twenty other people who were waiting for the train.

The group included a family of five from Germany, a young Australian woman who was traveling alone, and a number of other tourists speaking different languages we could not understand. They seemed happy, and we heard them say "Roma" many times. They appeared to be as anxious to get there as we were.

Our train was scheduled to arrive at 8:07 p.m., and we had about fifty minutes to wait. Having been informed about the "punctuality" of Italian trains, we were pleasantly surprised that the train arrived a few minutes early. It came to a stop with the engine right beside our platform. We assumed the first-class passenger car was directly behind the locomotive, so we lined up to board there. When the door opened, we hurled our hefty bags onto the train and jumped aboard. I was the first one onto the back section of the first car with DJ tagging along right behind me. The other tourists quickly followed our lead.

DJ noticed the seat numbers did not correspond with our tickets. DJ asked a man who was sitting in an aisle seat if we were in the right place. The man looked at our tickets and shook his head. "Wrong train," he said.

"What!?" I shouted, "Don't you mean the wrong car?"

"No, wrong train."

"Where is this train going?" DJ asked.

"Istanbul."

I bolted for the door, leaving DJ and all of our bags. I leaped off the bullet train, hoping to find a conductor or anyone who could help. Looking left, then right... there was no conductor or anyone left on Platform Five. But there was the engineer, perched high above in his seat. I ran up to the front of the locomotive to draw his attention.

Waving my arms, I blurted out, "Is this train going to Rome?" He gazed down and simply stared at me. He didn't say a word. Again, I yelled even louder, "IS THIS TRAIN GOING TO ROME?" He just shrugged.

All I could think of was Jennifer and Rob and Tamra in London. I had to act quickly. I screamed at the top of my lungs, "ROMA ... IS THIS TRAIN GOING TO ROMA!?"

Then he smiled at me. Finally, I thought, he heard me. And with a smirk, he said, "No Roma."

Now it was time to panic.

I raced back to the car, hoping DJ was making his way with all the bags to the exit. I reached the car, and suddenly the train doors shut. Right in my face! Not only was my husband still on the train behind closed doors, but he had all of our luggage and belongings. My euros. My credit card. My cell phone. My passport.

I started banging on the door. DJ watched me through the window, and I shouted once more at the engineer, "OPEN THIS DOOR! PLEASE! OPEN THIS DOOR!"

The engineer wasn't fazed in the least. He just

looked at me. I assumed he thought I was an outraged, crazy American woman. He might have been right about all of that.

Again, I yelled at the top of my lungs, "YOU OPEN THIS DOOR! MY HUSBAND IS ON THIS TRAIN!"

Then, at that moment, the door opened, and DJ tumbled out onto the ground with all of our bags. The other tourists heading to Rome also quickly exited. The German family, however, didn't make it out before the doors closed. The bullet train pulled out of the station, now on its way non-stop to Istanbul.

Within ten minutes, another train arrived. Before boarding, we asked someone, "Is this train going to Roma?" Assured that it was, we boarded. We worked our way to the first car and stored our luggage on a rack in the back of the car. Not able to find our seat numbers, we plopped down into two empty seats, hungry and exhausted, yet grateful to be on the rails and headed to Roma.

First-class service was non-existent for the entire trip. At that point, we really didn't care. At least we were heading in the right direction. Rome was just around the corner. DJ and I snuggled and attempted to sleep. Later, DJ told me how proud he was of me. "My calm and composed wife with a quiet demeanor," he said, "It was like you were transformed into a mother bear out to protect her cubs."

About twenty minutes before our arrival, a conductor finally asked to see our tickets. He said we were in the wrong seats and in the wrong car. We were, however, on the right train. The first-class section was one car back, he told us, and we could move if we wanted, but the food and wine service had already been stowed away. He said it would be easier and faster to exit the train if we stayed where we were. At least we would be in front of the line.

We pulled into the Roma Termini just before midnight, made our way through the train station, and found our pre-arranged driver who was awaiting our arrival. He whisked us off to the Marriott Grand Flora Hotel. On the way, we passed the Trevi Fountain and other sights we would enjoy tomorrow. But now, in the dark of the night, we felt embraced by Rome, the Eternal City. To be perfectly honest, we were mostly thrilled to not be headed to Istanbul.

A Pearl of Wisdom:
Let Your Voice Be Heard

The train station story made me realize that many of us have faced times in life when it seems every door is closed. As a result, we might just want to fade into the background. If we idly sit back and stay silent, we can become frustrated and confused. The question is: How will you confront life's obstacles and challenges head on?

Don't be afraid to speak up. Ask questions. Listen to your inner voice. Stay confident. And express yourself. Wherever life takes you—going through a divorce, confronting a serious illness, being abused or bullied, dealing with a work-related issue, or being left behind at the train station—let your voice be heard.

Chapter 16

Fly Me to the Moon

I HAD LONG IMAGINED Rome as a beautiful and romantic place steeped in history. Now sixty-three, I had the chance to make a two-day visit to this celebrated city and see for myself. We arrived at the Marriott Grand Hotel Flora on Via Vittorio Veneto well after midnight. Despite the late check in, the woman at the front desk was gracious and accommodating. Knowing our time in Rome would be short, she gave us good advice on how to maximize the few days we had in this beautiful city. She was optimistic that guided sightseeing arrangements could be made to fit our tight schedule. We were told to come to the lobby at 6:45 in the morning. While we slept, she arranged a whirlwind one-day, semi-private tour for the next day.

DJ and I were up before dawn, and we went to the rooftop terrace where we took in the spectacular views of the Eternal City. The Villa Borghese gardens and historic Roman walls were in sight. Reminders of its past are everywhere you turn in Rome. Ancient sites, museums and galleries, buildings and piazzas, and fountains from the Renaissance.

A limo driver met us in the lobby and whisked us off to the Roman Forum, where we met Jerry, the owner of the tour company, and Mindy, our guide. Jerry was a small, graying man in his fifties. He was gregarious and quick to smile. There was also a perceptible power about him. It was obvious that he was the man in charge. Mindy was a petite, attractive blonde and appeared to be in her thirties. She took orders from Jerry. Before we left on the tour, he pulled her aside and spoke with fervor and passion in Italian while waving his hands and noticeably instructing her. She seemed agitated and barked back at him. Jerry turned away quickly as if dismissing her.

We were introduced to a family of six from Malaysia who would be touring with us for the day. The family consisted of a man, his two wives, one teen, and two younger sons. We barely said hello before Jerry left and Mindy took off on foot toward the Forum. We all had to push ourselves to keep up with her. Time was tight. She knew it, and so did we. We had ten hours to explore the city, so there was no time to waste.

The Roman Forum was a marketplace that was the center of daily life in Rome for centuries. The Forum saw elections, public speeches, criminal trials, gladiator matches, and commercial activities. It is "the most celebrated marketplace in the entire world." More than 4.5 million sightseers tour this site each year.

Following our walk through the ruins, a new driver was summoned and picked us up in a different limo. The day was packed full of activity, including a visit to the Colosseum in the center of the city. The magnificent elliptical structure is built of travertine, tuff, and brick-faced concrete. One could imagine the armored gladiators and fierce lions battling each other with wild and uproarious crowds. *Thumbs up! Thumbs down!*

The Basilica of St. Mary—Our Lady of the Snow—was our next stop. This splendid cathedral is considered one of the most important Christian shrines in the world; it is dedicated to the Blessed Virgin Mary. Built in the fourth century AD, this basilica is believed to be one of the first Catholic churches in Rome.

Mindy was on the phone at various times, wheeling and dealing to get us into places with the least amount of wait time. We were on our way to have a sit-down meal at a restaurant when she suddenly received a call. She told us there had been a change in the day's schedule. She found out that our time to explore the Vatican had been moved up, and we needed to leave pronto. So much for a laid-back meal.

The young Malaysian boys expressed their displeasure. To keep the boys happy, the guide yielded to them and said we'd make a quick stop. DJ and I were thankful for that because we were famished. We galloped through a neighborhood, and Mindy rushed our party into a family-run deli to grab sandwiches to go.

Another limo and new driver appeared on the scene to transport our group to the Vatican. Our chauffeur deftly wove in and out of traffic and pulled the town car as close to the entrance as possible. It was early in the afternoon, and thousands of people were waiting in the blistering heat to get tickets to enter. We wondered how we could possibly avoid spending hours in line.

The tour guide ushered us through the crowded courtyard and into a building where fatigued tourists were patiently waiting. Alongside this group, another line of Vatican-goers was slowly making its way through a gated area. They too had been lingering for hours and appeared anxious to enter. Our guide informed us that those purchasing tickets at the window now had to make their way to the ticketed line to await their turns to enter. Then, she said, "Follow me and stay close together." We veered off around the two lengthy processions of tourist groups and skipped the lines. In a matter of minutes, our group was headed straight into the Vatican. Clearly, Jerry had connections in high places.

These hallowed grounds include numerous ornate galleries housing some of Italy's most treasured works of art. Paintings, sculptures, tapestries, and classical antiquities are everywhere you look. Inside the Vatican, we toured St. Peter's Basilica, its courtyards, and other buildings in the complex.

Our last stop at the Vatican was the Sistine Chapel. Before entering, women are required to cover their bare shoulders with a white cloth to show respect. The sanctuary is famous for Michelangelo's work with scenes from Genesis painted on the ceiling and *The Last Judgment* fresco hanging on the sanctuary's altar wall. Seeing the work of Michelangelo (*Il Divino* or The Divine One) was spellbinding. The Sistine Chapel is near the Raphael Rooms, the stunning frescoes of Botticelli and Perugino, the work of Bernini, and other great masters of the Renaissance.

Before Mindy said goodbye after the Vatican tour, she extended an invitation from Jerry to all of us to have dinner that evening. It was to make up for the lunch we had missed, she said. It was an unexpected gesture, and we gratefully accepted. Before taking us to the ristorante, our driver chauffeured us around the city, pointing out the Piazza di Spagna with the Spanish Steps, and Trevi Fountain, and other attractions.

At the ristorante, we found a large dining table outside on the sidewalk. It was adorned with a red and white checkered tablecloth, red cloth napkins, a bouquet of fresh flowers, eight table settings, glassware, and wine stems—ready and waiting for the Malaysian family, DJ, and me.

A waitress handed each of us a menu, but in a few minutes, she circled back and took the menus away. Pointing to a window, she said, "Jerry decided he would order for your table." Jerry, the owner, waved at us through the window and lifted his glass in salute.

Our server brought out several carafes of Chianti and filled our glasses. Several waiters then brought out the appetizers—bruschetta, fried ravioli, and antipasto—and then came a tossed Caesar salad with anchovy dressing. The main course included a variety of meats—beef, chicken, and fish—and large platters of roasted vegetables, gnocchi, and several kinds of pasta. The incredible feast was topped off with a choice of dessert—tiramisu, cannoli, or coconut gelato.

As everyone was finishing their meal, Jerry asked the driver to take the Malaysian family back to their hotel. As soon as we said our goodbyes to our new friends, we expected another driver to appear and take us back to the hotel, but the waitress came to us and said, "Jerry would like to invite the two of you to stay and have a glass of wine with him." We, of course, obliged and went in to meet our host and benefactor.

"Please, have a seat," he said, "I couldn't help but notice the two of you. I'm interested in hearing your story."

So, we shared a bit of our lives with him. As we talked, Jerry would become distracted from time to time by one of the three cell phones in front of him. DJ and I later surmised from the numerous conversations we had overheard that one phone was for business, one for his wife and kids, and the third for his paramours. He would occasionally snap his fingers, and the bartender, waiters, the hostess, and other employees would jump and do his bidding.

One of his paramours, a young and very pretty

twenty-something waitress named Cecelia, was summoned to our table. With a noticeable glint in his eye, Jerry grabbed her around the waist and introduced her as his "niece." She simply chuckled, grinned, and rolled her big brown eyes as to let us know that was not the case.

As we were finishing a glass of vino, I asked Jerry for a restaurant recommendation the next night. I mentioned that, "I love this place, but we'd like to experience another one of your favorite restaurants for our last night in Rome." Without a word, he reached for one of his three phones, speed-dialed a number, and began speaking in Italian.

After seven or eight minutes, he said to us, "I've made a reservation for the two of you for tomorrow night at Antico Forno Marucci. Be there at eight o'clock. Oh, and I have taken the liberty to order your dinner and the wine for your last night in Rome. My good friend Bobby owns the restaurant. He'll take very good care of you."

Jerry wrote down the name of the restaurant and the address then handed it to DJ. We thanked him for everything and told him we had to get back to our hotel.

"Your hotel is only five to six blocks away from here," he insisted, "I'll walk you there." Next, he informed the staff around him that Cecelia, his "niece," would be going with the three of us. She was summoned; they embraced; and we all headed out toward the Grand Flora Hotel.

After a few short blocks, Jerry told us the hotel was

only two blocks ahead. Then he said he and Cecelia were heading to his office, which was in the opposite direction. We thanked him again for a wonderful day and evening. We hugged each other and said goodbye. They wandered off arm-in-arm, and DJ and I concluded that Jerry was both the Godfather and Don Juan of the neighborhood.

We enjoyed an early breakfast on the rooftop terrace the next morning and headed out on our own to explore the shops and galleries in the area. The first place we stopped, though, was the Pantheon.

Originally a pagan temple built during the reign of Augustus in AD 126, it was dedicated as a church in AD 609. Fortunately, this structure was saved from destruction when Rome fell in the Middle Ages. It later became a house of worship for the underprivileged. The building holds the record for the world's largest, unreinforced concrete dome. It was a place of simple beauty, but it was even more stunning to me than the opulent and gold-laced Basilica of St. Peter's.

After admiring this extraordinary structure for nearly an hour, we noticed congregants were entering the church and sitting in the wooden pews. A bell rang and an announcement was made, first in Italian and then in English. The recorded message stated, "The church will be closing in ten minutes for Sunday Mass and communion. Visitors are welcome to return in one hour as soon as services are over." Tourists began leaving, but DJ and I decided to stay for the service. We both grew up in Protestant families, so we were both intrigued at the idea of participating in a Catholic Latin Mass in the oldest surviving church in Rome.

We walked toward the front of the church and sat in the third pew, close to the aisle. Before the service began, two young acolytes lit the candles on the dais and the altar. Two priests had entered from behind the altar. One was obviously the most senior, and the other was an attractive young man who looked to be in his thirties. He could easily have been mistaken for a young Antonio Banderas.

The young priest walked into the church proper, approached an Italian woman, and handed her what appeared to be a Bible. The next thing I knew, Father Antonio Banderas came over and stopped where DJ and I were sitting. He greeted me warmly, handed me the readings for the Mass, and asked, "Madam, can you read this?" The words were in English, so of course I could. I thought, "How sweet of him. He assumed I was American and wanted me to be able to follow along with the Latin Mass."

I said, "Yes, thank you!" And he handed me the booklet.

When he was gone, DJ leaned over and said, "Judy, I'll take your picture during Mass."

"Sweetheart, I don't think it's appropriate to take pictures during the services," I said.

"What do you mean? How many times in life do you get asked to read at a Mass, let alone at the Pantheon in Rome, Italy?"

Then it hit me. Father Antonio Banderas had just

asked me to stand up there at the dais, in front of all of these people in the oldest church in Rome, and read out loud! And I had just agreed to do it!

My heart thumped, and my mouth got dry. I was terrified. I looked down at the readings. I could tell they were in English, but the words were fuzzy. I couldn't see them clearly.

"DJ, I can't go up there! I didn't bring my glasses. You'll have to do this."

He could tell I was terrified, and he knew there was a very good possibility I would stammer and stutter over the blurred words. So, he agreed to go up in my place, to sit with the two priests and the young Italian woman until it was his time to read. Once he stepped up to the dais, I pulled out my cell phone and took his photo. He was a blur to me at this distance, but thankfully there is autofocus.

Later that night we taxied to the Antico Forno Marucci. It was a long cab ride, and it took us into a neighborhood that felt like the real Italy—narrow streets, apartment-style living, a working-class neighborhood.

Bobby greeted us as soon as we walked through the doors, welcoming us as if we were family. The large dining room was empty with the exception of one man sitting alone eating pizza.

Bobby and his waitress, Patricia, hovered over us all evening long. Bobby did all the talking, describing in detail every course and how each food item was prepared. Patricia, with a broad smile, quietly served every course. She did not speak English, or so we thought. You never know for sure. They served more than five courses of the best Italian food I've ever had. Their hospitality was the best. We laughed and enjoyed each other's company. After an hour or so, we looked around to see couples and families piling into the restaurant. Ten o'clock on a Sunday night and the place was packed. The atmosphere was festive and vibrant. No Michelin star restaurant could have matched the experience we had. Great food, great service, delicious vino, and a night we'll never forget.

Being in this restaurant and in this neighborhood gave us a glimpse of another face of Rome. It felt real, down to earth. I was struck by the complexity of this city. In many ways, it held up a mirror to my own life.

Rome is a modern city, with antiquities that date back thousands of years. Stories within stories. The relics of the Roman Empire—its ruins and art—provide answers to this ancient civilization and show where this modern city sprang from. In today's Rome, we saw both prosperity and poverty. The haves and the have-nots, the troubles and joys embodied in one place. There is a sort of cultural soul-searching taking place in broad daylight.

Affluence was abundant. In tourist areas, many streets were lined lavishly with luxury hotels, fine dining restaurants, and boutiques with designer fashions, high quality leather goods, and fine jewelry. The city had high-end art galleries featuring the paintings and sculptures of recognized and emerging artists. Their works of art sold for thousands of euros. In contrast, as we walked out of the Pantheon that Sunday, the adjoining Piazza della Rotonda held an open market filled with many vendors selling their merchandise in a festival-like atmosphere. I noticed talented, yet-to-break-through artists waiting to be discovered and eager to sell their prized original pieces for a fraction of the price of those showing in upscale galleries.

When we had arrived in Rome, the conductor gave us directions for exiting the station, and he asked, "Do you have a driver here to meet you?" Fortunately, we did. Then, he warned us to make our way through the crowd quickly and find our driver. He said, "Pickpockets, drug traffickers and druggies, and panhandlers are waiting and ready for tourists."

Everywhere in Rome, it seemed that men were in charge and women were subservient. Jerry with his three phones, wheeling and dealing and taking charge of everyone and everything around him with a snap of his fingers. I thought about the young waitress, Cecelia, and how she reacted to his demands. I thought about Mindy and Patricia at Antico Forno. Women, it seemed, are not to be heard and not to lead. They are to serve.

I also remembered the lines of commoners and other tourists waiting for hours in the baking sun to get into the Vatican. Those with money or connections were dropped off by limos, passed the lines of thousands of people, moved to the front of the crowd, and found doors opened immediately for them.

Inside the Vatican, we were stunned to see the thousands and thousands of artifacts crammed inside in the museums. Likely billions of dollars of art treasures! People with little—people—who struggle each day, waited for hours and were eager to get through the doors to see the riches.

Money may buy things, but it's not what I truly value in life.

Rome's different mirror images made me look through my own rear-view mirror and examine my life. I've been blessed by God and my angels. All my life I've been chosen, and because of this, I've chosen to step more consciously in becoming who I am.

Going all the way back when I was sixteen years old, I was chosen and elected to a position of leadership with the Kayettes service-learning organization. I was chosen to create Children's Discovery House for Methodist Medical Center at the age of twenty-eight. I was chosen at thirty-four to lead a foundation and spearhead an emerging movement about healthy communities. I was chosen to lead an effort to create emPowerU, an innovative place that coached thousands of young people from all walks of life about the value of an education and community involvement. I was chosen by loving friends and wonderful workmates. And I was even chosen by Father Antonio Banderas to read scripture in the oldest church in Rome. I was chosen by the birds in Sedona.

Divorce chose me. As a result, many years later, the love of my life chose me.

Cancer chose me, too. Ultimately, the blessing is that I was chosen to have a second chance to live.

All these blessings and all these people are things money cannot buy. Even divorce and cancer were blessings in disguise. All of these are the real treasures worthy of my gratitude.

So, as I think about what's most important, I'm struck by the everyday, ordinary things that bring joy in life.

Hugging your child. Sharing a meal with family and friends. Reading a good book. Breathing in acts of kindness. Helping others. Taking long walks. Feeling the sun on your face. Sitting by a fire. Dancing in the rain. Watching a sunset. Seeing the beauty in our planet. Making memories. Saying grace.

These are the blessings that make life extraordinary. It's soul-filled living.

We left the restaurant very late that night and had a little trouble getting a cab. We had no limo this evening, and we didn't mind at all. We eventually made it back to our hotel on Via Vittorio Veneto.

As we stepped out of the cab at the hotel, we heard a man playing an electric keyboard and singing Frank Sinatra songs. Several other couples were sitting at tables on the sidewalk listening. Then DJ took my hand and we started to dance to *Fly Me to the Moon.* A perfect ending to a perfect day!

A Pearl of Wisdom:

Expect the Unexpected

Tap into the world that surrounds you. Always be prepared for the possibility those unexpected blessings in life have been chosen for you. These blessings are all there waiting to happen through you. You'll experience a depth of love, joy, peace, and fulfillment you've never imagined. And, sometimes, you may experience challenging times that turn out to be some of the greatest blessings of all.

And remember this: Never leave home without your glasses.

Chapter 17

Just Breathe

THIS IS A CHAPTER I never wanted to write. But I knew I had to. It was the last chapter I wrote, and it was the most difficult.

The manuscript of this book was essentially finished, and I had already begun shopping it around to several publishers. It was the story I wanted to tell, and it followed me from love lost to love found; from cancer to recovery; from joy to sorrow and back to joy. Writing this book had been a godsend because it helped me process all of those challenges, and it crystalized meaning and purpose.

My life has been touched by God and the presence of His benevolent angels. I have sensed them while going through my divorce and when my parents passed away. They appeared in Sedona as my relationship

with DJ was being blessed from above. I felt their presence when I battled breast cancer. I know I never would
have finished this manuscript without them.

At no time did I sense their presence more than
this past month when the unthinkable happened. My
son Hayden was killed.

On July 11, 2021, DJ and I had just returned from a late
afternoon swim off the dock and were soaking up time
together inside our lake cabin when DJ's cell phone
rang. It was his son, Ryan. Ryan asked if I was there.
And then he broke the news.

Not grasping his words, we repeated over and
over, "No, that can't be."

"It's not possible," I wailed, "What are you saying?"

Ryan repeated the news. "Hayden passed away."

Ryan gave us the details. The police had come to
inform us at our home in Kansas City, but we were at
the lake. So, they went door to door in the neighborhood, and one of our neighbors had Ryan's contact
information. The police immediately drove to Ryan's
house and informed him there had been a motorcycle
accident. Hayden had been killed. He was only thirty
years old.

A few minutes after Ryan's call, Hayden's sister
and brother called. Jordan and Ryan were together in
St Louis. Jordan had been informed by the Kirkwood
police, and the news was more than she could take.

Eight months pregnant, she collapsed to the floor. She couldn't hear any other words the police said. She and her husband drove to her brother and sister-in-law's house to tell them so they could plan on how to break it to me. They even discussed driving down to the lake to tell us face to face, but they realized with a five-hour drive, the news might travel faster than they could reach me.

When I received their call, I was already melting down. They knew instantly that I knew, and we all sobbed together over the phone.

Hayden had texted me a couple of hours before his fatal accident. He was keeping me posted about his plans to move the following week. His life, it seemed, was coming together. Now it was gone. It all came as a shock to me. Over and over. But I barely had time to think, to let it sink in, before I had to face reality and make important decisions.

The police had left a number for me to contact the hospital chaplain at Mosaic Life Care. The chaplain offered his condolences and words of comfort over the phone, and he said that Hayden had noted on his driver's license that he wanted to be an organ donor. With my permission, the chaplain said, someone from the Midwest Transplant Network would contact me. I agreed, and it was only minutes later I received a call from the Transplant Network.

There was a barrage of questions, and my head was swimming. I paced back and forth through the entire call, answering the questions to the best of my ability.

Time was of the essence, I was gently told, because a person's organs and tissue must be harvested within twenty-four hours of death for them to be viable. Then they asked me to give my permission to transport Hayden's body to the Organ Transplant Center.

I knew my son's soul was no longer in his physical body, but that didn't make it any easier. I realized Hayden was giving a gift or multiple gifts to others for a better quality of life and quite possibly for life itself. That's what Hayden wanted. I gave my permission.

Hayden had his ups and downs, but he rose above the challenging times and was on the right path. He was a kind and gentle soul, had a big heart, and could light up any room with his contagious smile and laugh. I recognized when he was turning five years old that he marched to the beat of a different drummer, and that's what made him so special to our family. Many people, some I did not even know, came to me to relate how Hayden made them feel special. That was Hayden.

Does it hurt? Yes. More than any pain I've ever experienced. More than divorce and more than cancer. The death of a child is traumatizing and complicated. It's true that a person wouldn't hurt this much from such a loss unless he or she was blessed to love that person so much. And how blessed I am to have loved Hayden so deeply that it makes saying goodbye so hard. Thank God, I was given this gift.

After getting the news, DJ and I were sitting on the back porch at the cabin in complete silence later that night. Neither of us felt like speaking. Hundreds of cicadas were buzzing in the background. I was having difficulty catching my breath, and I told DJ I couldn't breathe. I was both grief-stricken and in shock, and I called out to Hayden and pleaded that I wanted just one more hug, and then I expressed to him out loud that I needed a sign that he was okay. I listened to the voice of my soul. At that moment, a gift he had made and presented to me last October popped into my mind. I shouted out to DJ that I knew his sign. Quite literally, it was his sign. It was a painting he had created for me.

The wooden sign displayed a single dandelion with some of the seeds scattering to the wind. Below the dandelion were two simple words. *Just Breathe*. It had to be his sign.

After my brother Doug died of COVID and other complications in October of 2020, Hayden gave me the painted sign as an early Christmas present and as a way to bring me strength during our family's time of loss. The family had gathered at our house in Kansas City following Doug's services. After an emotional day, Hayden pointed to the painting and reminded me to just breathe. He placed it against the fireplace in the family room where everyone could see.

Fifteen minutes after recalling Hayden's sign on the porch that night, confirmation was sent through a text message from my niece Caitlyn, Doug's daughter. It read: "I'm holding you in my arms in this exact moment. These are the only words I can muster to say. Hayden gave you a message when Dad died. He told you to "Just Breathe" through his painting. He's asking you to do the same now. Just breathe. Breathe with Hayden. He's right next to you."

I struggled to sleep that night. Once I did, I suddenly woke up. I was completely wide-awake and I heard my son's voice. This was real and not imagined. He sounded like he was standing right next to me. I could not believe what I had just heard.

"Just breathe, Mom. Just breathe," he said.

I remember crying and shaking uncontrollably. DJ comforted me and held me in his arms. At that moment after hearing Hayden's voice, I knew he was alright and that his soul had been released to heaven.

I talked with each one of my kids, Ryan and Jordan, separately that morning and related the story. When Jordan heard the story, she gasped and cried. She said it had been a rough morning, and she was almost hyperventilating. Her husband rubbed her back and told her, "Just breathe, Jordan. Just breathe."

When Jordan and I made these connections to the sign, our healing had begun.

DJ and I spent the rest of the morning packing and preparing for the task that lay ahead—going to the funeral home to plan his services. While DJ loaded the car, I worked inside. Suddenly, he ran into the cabin and said, "Judy, you need to come outside. I think you're going to want to see this."

I walked outside, and there it was resting on the patio stone—a black and blue butterfly.

"It flew into my chest and circled around me," DJ said, "Then, the butterfly landed nearby and, for the longest time, sat there with its wings spread. It wouldn't leave."

We watched it for about fifteen minutes. DJ went inside, and I stayed with it. Then, all of a sudden, the butterfly flew toward me and completely encircled me as close as possible. It was as if the butterfly were sending a heavenly hug from my son, and it seemed as though the black and blue creature wanted to stay. In fact, more than twenty minutes had passed, and it remained close by me for some time longer. Another sign that Hayden was in God's care.

The next day, DJ and I arrived at the funeral home in St. Joseph. My son and daughter drove from St. Louis to join us, as did Hayden's dad, Larry, and his wife, Mary, from KC. Together, we planned the service. At times, I would think this couldn't be possible. A cloud of numbness surrounded me while we made funeral arrangements for the youngest of my children. Somehow, we all managed to get through the meeting. I can only give credit to God for the strength He gave to all of us that day.

Just a few weeks before Hayden passed, I decided to rummage through several trunks that had been gathering dust and had been hidden away for more than a decade or two. The trunks were filled with memories of each of my kids: photographs, school awards, mementos, cards, artwork, and other keepsakes. Who would have anticipated the photos would now be assembled for a slide show at the family visitation on Thursday night and the funeral the following day?

At Hayden's service, Ryan and Jordan shared their thoughts about their little brother with a great deal of courage from the dais that day. Ryan mentioned how "deeply selfless and caring" Hayden was and how he always saw the good in other people.

Jordan talked about how much he had leaned on us for guidance in his life. "Now the thing is, the tables have turned," she said, "We are going to look to him for guidance and advice when we make our final crossing."

We were surrounded by the love of family and friends for that first week, and their compassion and caring continue to this day. Comfort food was delivered to feed those who came by our house every night. Fresh flowers and plants, cards and notes, and phone calls and texts were sent from loved ones nearby as well as far and wide. Memorial gifts were designated to the Friends of the Animal Shelter because Hayden was such a lover of animals. Additional gifts were made to other local charities.

My family and I have faced difficult struggles in life. But we realize we can't chase away our troubles and adversities. By embracing the power of our faith, we've gained the wisdom and strength of character to confront those hard times when they come.

The rare black and blue butterfly reappeared a number of other times after Hayden's passing. At one of those times, Karen and Mark were with us. We had just pulled into the garage and had exited the car. I noticed a butterfly resting on the concrete driveway behind the car—the same black and blue one. I leaned over to place my opened hand down next to the creature, and it crawled into my palm.

A couple of weeks before Hayden's death, Jordan had made a trip back to KC for a baby shower and to visit our family in June. She insisted Hayden come down on his day off. She wanted him to see her in her expectant state. In fact, she wouldn't take no for an answer, so he drove down on his motorcycle to his dad's house and spent the day with them. It was the last time she saw Hayden, and it was so clear that he was happy with the direction his life had taken. Hayden told her that day, "You don't even look pregnant, Joey. You just look like you have pillows stuffed in your stomach." With three Ryans in our family, he also suggested she name her son Hayden.

On Jordan's birthday, she received the best gift ever. She gave birth to her son. His name is Jackson Hayden Mica.

I've experienced angels in my life in different forms. They are there if we open our eyes and minds to see.

Our angels are constantly watching over us. Listen

to their guidance and the voice of your soul. These grace-filled moments can be life-changing. The choice is ours.

God now holds my son in His everlasting arms while we wait to be with him someday in the future. What may seem like years to us now will turn out to be only a moment before we see each other again. And on that day, Hayden will light the way and greet his loved ones with his contagious smile and open arms to show us where we're going. I can't wait to see him. And I know he can't wait to show this new path to his family and friends.

Until that day, I tell myself ... just breathe.

A Pearl of Wisdom:

Keep Hope Alive

The morning after hearing the dreadful news about Hayden, I went up to my writing space in the loft to pack my computer and other papers as we were preparing to head home to Kansas City. While opening my desk drawer to search for a pen and notepad, an unfamiliar pink memo sheet lay face up and had the words *Keep Hope Alive* printed on it in my handwriting. Below these three words I had referenced two scriptures: John 3:16 and Ezekiel 37:5.

John 3:16 is likely the most quoted Bible verse of all and one of my favorites since childhood. The verse, "For God so loved the world, He gave His one and only son, that whoever believes in Him, shall have eternal life," was spoken by Jesus to Nicodemus about being born again. He was emphasizing the transformation of a person's earthly life into a heavenly everlasting life. The freed butterfly symbolizes this transformation of a new creation and resurrection.

In the other scripture, Ezekiel 37:5 prophesizes about dry bones (death) and new life. "This is what the Sovereign Lord says to these bones: I will make breath enter you, and you will come to life." I believe the Lord has placed new breath in Hayden, and his soul has been resurrected in heaven.

Losing a child is unimaginable, but God works in mysterious ways to help us find the courage to face our darkest moments and discover splendor from this wounded space. God's love never departs from us. I also know Hayden's love will forever surround me.

In those moments of acknowledging the deeper meanings of Hayden's "Just Breathe" painting and seeing the black and blue butterfly, it encouraged me to keep my hope alive. Both the wooden sign and the butterfly spoke of transformation, renewal, and resurrection for eternal life as promised by God through His son, Jesus. In fact, I take refuge not only believing it to be so, but also counting on it.

Chapter 18

Dancing in the Labyrinth of Life

HAYDEN'S DEATH—AND THE GRIEF that followed and the mourning that continues—provided me with an unexpected insight: that life is full of journeys we did not choose to make. Some journeys—divorce, cancer, death—choose us. They are arduous and painful, and sometimes they test our faith. Yet it is faith that saves us, along with the love of others.

When I was going through cancer, I hit new lows. I endured two major surgical procedures right from the start—the first was a double mastectomy, with the start of the reconstruction process, including multiple saline injections. The second came four weeks later to remove a temporary implant because of a life-threatening infection. Two more major surgeries followed. The third one was to put a new temporary expander/implant in my chest and begin the weekly injection rounds for reconstruction. The fourth surgery was necessary to remove the two temporary devices and replace those implants with my new permanent breasts. The last phase of the reconstruction process required the fifth and sixth surgeries to do tissue grafting: one focused on taking tissue from my abdomen and the last one, from my back.

During this time, when days were dark and the pain was real, I sometimes had to dig deep inside my soul. My spiritual faith is everything. It is my foundation. Whenever I hit one of those dark moments, I would circle back to my faith, bonded through prayer and meditation. Other times I would imagine the calmness, serenity, and love in the sacred space created for me and DJ at the close of the Wisdom Gathering at the Colorado Chautauqua in Boulder. That was when, just two days after I was diagnosed, we were surrounded by the compassion of so many spiritual supporters. We had just begun our journey. Now, more than seven years and six major surgeries later, I am cancer-free.

While recovering, I connected with nature by taking short meditative walks. I listened to music and read devotionals like *Grace for the Morning* and *Jesus Is Calling*. And all along this journey, through our struggle, DJ and I learned to dance again. It was dancing that helped me heal, that helped me find love, that helped me feel alive again. So... we danced.

We danced to *Stand by Me* in a hotel room in Anaheim. We danced in the moonlight in the courtyard outside McCormick and Schmick's on the Plaza in Kansas City, where a street musician dedicated a song to us—the Righteous Brothers' *(You're My) Soul and Inspiration*—and other couples got up and joined us.

We danced in the sunlight out in the middle of a street in St. Augustine, Florida. We danced on a sidewalk in Rome at midnight while a man played Frank Sinatra songs. We danced with friends to the healing music of Three Trees at the Wisdom Gathering in Chautauqua Park. We danced at Jordan and Ryan's wedding. And with full hearts, we danced with our grandchildren as they came into our lives.

DJ and I danced on the Olive Oyl to Michael McDonald, The Doobie Brothers, and Phil Collins while we were moored in Paradise Cove at Table Rock Lake. We've even danced in the rain. And now, I'm re-learning and daring to dance again with DJ while holding Hayden in my heart.

To this day, we dance together every chance we get. We have traveled to our favorite places on this planet, and we have faced death and danced in the labyrinth of life.

And with every dance, my heart has been full of gratitude.

With my struggles with divorce and cancer over, I

was given a gift, a second chance at life—as a woman, a mother, a wife, and a grandmother. Now with the death of Hayden, I feel as if God and my angels are closer than ever—giving me the strength and faith to carry on. And I can just imagine my son dancing with joy in Heaven.

I asked God, the Source of the Universe, to help me discover what's next and imagine what's possible. Help me to make a difference in whatever form it takes. To gently lead, to write, to speak words of wisdom I have learned from life's experiences. To reach people with kindness and compassion one at a time.

DJ is my partner in life. He is a source of inspiration and my soul twin on this journey of discovery. Our collective intent is to touch the hearts and souls of others as our unbreakable bond and great love for one another continues to merge and embrace the fullness of life at the deepest level.

A Pearl of Wisdom:

Profess Your Intentions

There are a number of signs in our home. They are pieces of art with words of inspiration and wisdom. They remind us of important truths.

Jordan gave me one of those pieces of art as a birthday gift recently. It is a framed window, about twenty-four inches wide and thirty inches tall, and it hangs above my writing desk in the loft at our lake cabin. The piece depicts a contemporary design of an oak tree with deep roots. One side of the tree is full of leaves, and on the other side the leaves are fluttering away and transforming into what appears to be birds and butterflies. These prophetic words are painted in white lettering on glass:

WINGS
to show you what
you can become

ROOTS
to remind you
where you're from

On my own path of discovery, I've found my life to be deeply rooted in transformational experiences that have been beautiful, joyful, and, at times, shattering. All these soulful encounters have led to what I am choosing to become.

Life is filled with abundance should we choose

to see it that way. When your days seem darkest and chaotic, have the courage and confidence to set your intentions and begin to re-script your life by imagining what's possible. Change your mindset and embrace the possibilities showing up through you. With God's grace, seek the life that is waiting for you.

There is another sign in our lake cabin. It is on the porch, a reminder to us as we leave home and enter the world each day. It reads:

> IF YOU THINK SUNSHINE BRINGS HAPPINESS,
> THEN YOU HAVEN'T DANCED IN THE RAIN.

Epilogue

In the spring of 2012, I was asked to deliver the commencement address at North Central Missouri College of Trenton, Missouri. Although I've often been called upon to speak in public, I am a natural introvert, and the thought of standing in front of all those young faces and their families made me nervous for weeks.

As I considered what I would say to those graduates, I recalled a similar time when I was invited to deliver one of the keynote addresses at the National Quest Conference for Malcolm Baldrige National Quality Award winners in Washington, DC. There would be three or four times as many people in the audience as there were in my hometown back in Kansas. Two weeks before the conference, I woke up one night fretting about facing such a large audience.

On my nightstand was a women's devotional Bible. I picked it up and let the pages fall where they may. It opened to a woman's story about her concern for giving an important speech. The devotional ended with Proverbs 18:16, which calls out God's intention for you to speak to great men. It was at that moment I knew that, no matter what I said at the conference, God would have my back. The knowledge that I was never alone has guided me ever since.

I related that story to the graduates of North Central Missouri College. And I told them another story, too.

When I was sixteen years old in the summer of 1969, I attended a weeklong Kayettes Leadership Camp in Topeka, Kansas. The Kayettes was a statewide student leadership and service organization for high school girls, and, on the first day of the camp, we heard from its founder, Wanda May Vinson.

I had never been more stirred by a speaker, and, more than fifty years later, I can still see her standing there in front of a hundred young women speaking to us in a voice that reached our souls, inspiring us to engage in our world.

She shared so much with us that day, but to be honest, I remember only one thing she said. It was a quote from the nineteenth century Unitarian clergyman Edward Everett Hale, who wrote:

I may only be one,
But I am one.
I cannot do everything,

But I can do some things.
What I can do,
I ought to do.
And what I ought to do,
By the grace of God,
I will do!

Ms. Vinson's stirring speech and Mr. Hale's powerful words still resonate with me today.

When you deliver a commencement address, you hope to impart something meaningful to those young people. You hope that perhaps they will find among your words a pearl of wisdom to latch onto, to hold for even just a little while.

When we consider our life's journey, we should think about what is possible and the choices we make. To create an extraordinary life, we must choose wisely. If we do, we ourselves might be chosen to lead, to show the way.

A String of Wisdom Pearls
Find Inner Peace and Guidance to Re-script Your Life

Joseph Campbell said, "We must be willing to get rid of the life we've planned, so as to have the life that is waiting for us."

The life I'd planned was no longer possible. The impending divorce compelled me to redesign what was then a broken life. No matter what hardships or heartaches you may go through, I discovered there are always new opportunities ready to unfold. These new openings create a chance to both learn and unlearn how you re-script your life from the present to the future with its infinite possibilities.

Moving forward takes patient persistence in order to heal and learn the lessons awaiting you. Ask God for strength and inner guidance. Dare to believe better days are ahead, while asking yourself: What desired change do you want for your life? What is your intention? What do you aspire to accomplish in this lifetime? How you answer those questions will shape how you live your life! Your existence may take a surprisingly new direction.

With boldness and courage, you can rebuild your life. It requires transforming those self-limiting thoughts and attitudes that hold you back. Instead, live a life of discovery, love, joy, faith, and wisdom. Find the strength to be the architect of your life in moving forward. *Be intentional!*

And remember: When you have the chance to sit it out or dance, I hope you *Dare to Dance Again*!

Encourage Others

Raw emotions would well up inside me during my divorce. Not knowing what the future held for me and my kids, there were many days I just felt numb. In my confusion of what was happening, comical moments like the one with Maddie would lift my spirits. Mostly, day brighteners occurred when my friends and family unexpectedly reached out during particularly fragile and chaotic days. On that cold, wintry Wednesday in February, that's just what my aunt did. She expressed her deep love and concern not just that day, but throughout my ordeal.

Although my Aunt Martha passed away some years ago, her encouragement, compassion, and caring are still felt today. Reach out to people in their time of need, and when things seem to be okay. You never know what a person may be going through, and your presence and reassurance may boost someone's life.

I once read a brief devotional passage called *Gravity at Work,* written by Sharon Mahoe. It was very fitting: "Encouragement. Doesn't sound like much, but it's everything. Send some encouragement today. You'll be a part of someone's memories for a long, long time."

Believe in a Higher Power

Dying is a sacred journey. Sitting at my parents' bedsides as they each actively went through the process was agonizing and sorrowful, but I'll always cherish those moments. As I reflected on their lives in those last few hours, I recounted how they lived long and blessed existences. They touched so many people with their love of humankind, generosity, joys and sorrows, and the example they set for others to embrace the fullness of life.

I believe that our angels are meant to guide and provide loving support during our time on this Earth. No doubt my angels did so as my parents were dying. My angels were present, and they confirmed my parents' souls were liberated. Bertha and Marvin had both blissfully entered heaven as our family witnessed indescribable celebrations of their departures. My mother and father's spirits filled every inch of the sky as the angelic birds departed. I felt the weight of their love being released to those of us left behind. To this day, my parents' love continues to envelop me and deeply touch my soul.

Our guardian angels provide grace-filled guidance, protection, and comfort to us on an unending basis. They send signs and messages that are personal and recognizable just for you. It is consoling, uplifting, and reassuring to know that through His angels, God sheds His love and mercy on His children.

Like Jordan shared when she discovered a sign on the day she sat at her grandfather's bedside, "Life is better when you believe (in a higher power)."

Stay Open to the Possibilities

Life can change when you least expect it. I know it did for me. More than a decade earlier, I had resigned and relegated myself to staying single for the rest of my life. Now, all of a sudden, I felt like a teenager who was giddy and head over heels with my first love. But I wasn't sixteen years old. I was soon to be a sixty-one-year-old woman, and I was a person, quite frankly, not expecting to fall in love. Let alone to find the love of my life.

Trust me. As I came to realize after meeting DJ, true love can happen even in your twilight years. I will say that during the twelve years I was alone, I discovered who I was beyond the conventional life roles people saw me in: a mom, a daughter, a divorcée, a friend, a professional career woman, a civic leader, and a woman of faith. With life's struggles, heartaches, and unexpected joys, I matured into someone who was learning to re-script my life. Sometimes you just have to wait for the right timing. At this point in my life, it was not just about the timing. It was about being open to new ways of thinking and being.

Take a chance. Fully engage in life. Be aware of what is happening around you. By being wholly and abundantly present and having the courage to change or take a chance, you open yourself up to creating new opportunities for something positive to occur in your life. Something you may never have expected just might be waiting to happen. Stay open to the possibilities!

Find Joy and Laughter

Noticing DJ's readiness to laugh at himself was heart-warming. What could have been an embarrassing and tense time on our third date actually became a bonding moment for us.

No matter what happens in your life, find spontaneous joy in those embarrassing, yet precious moments. When you have the courage to laugh at yourself, you gain a whole new perspective on the world and the people around you. Celebrate your life by making room for unconstrained joy and laughter.

Uncovering the rapture of laughter really does make a difference by touching one's soul. Not only will it brighten and uplift your day, it will likely cheer up someone else's heart.

And remember: Finding humor in something as simple as not recognizing the difference between the radio's volume control and ignition buttons can spark a special connection and actually help you dial in to another person.

Be Open to Signs and Messages

DJ and I have experienced a number of amazing, life-changing events. Those occasions have lifted our spirits as our angels have inspired, guided, watched over, and protected us. We know for certain that these experiences are more than coincidences.

Have you ever had a sign, message, or missive placed in front of you? Whether a natural wonder, a piece of artwork, a sermon, song lyrics or a musical composition that speaks to you, a vivid dream, or some other communique that has an underlying significant meaning, your guardian angels are the gentle voice of your soul. Watch and listen for them!

Too often, we get distracted in the busy-ness of everyday life and miss the messages and signs that are directed at us. Pay attention, or you will easily overlook the blessings and the grace-filled guidance that is there for you.

Love Unconditionally

As in this "Judy Moment," love makes doing even the everyday ordinary, and sometimes challenging tasks liberating for your soul. Love each other. Serve each other. Accept one another.

When you find a partner who loves and accepts you with all your "Judy Moments," you unlock the key to one's heart in spite of the other person's imperfections and shortcomings; it's more than just tolerating those embarrassing and awkward moments that happen to all of us. It's about embracing someone's faults and weaknesses—big and small.

You may just find those occurrences can even lead to a source of joy and delight. When you can do that, you will discover a deeply felt unconditional love and an unbreakable, shatterproof bond that will get you through the more problematic life challenges that come your way. Love unconditionally.

Oh, and remember: It's best not to put banana peels down your drain.

Embrace Life to the Fullest

Living your life to the fullest is contrary to what many people may think. Some would say it applies to only experiencing good things. Actually, I believe it can happen in many ways regardless of what your current situation is or past circumstances have been. Even when you face pain, sadness, illness, and/or loss, you can dig deep within your soul to find an appreciation for life and living. Living fully means you embrace all of life, which includes how you gratefully appreciate the good times as well as how you face the more challenging ones.

In all situations, you have the opportunity to learn and grow. Sometimes, that means you must unlearn what you've learned to fully heal your heart, your body, and your soul. If you tap into your inner guidance and live by faith, you can reinvigorate your life with an abundance of healing, joyfulness, serenity, and love.

As DJ says: "When life gets tough, which will happen, you have a choice. You can approach the situation with love, humility, and gratitude or with bitterness and a victim mentality. I choose to embrace life with love. Live life to the fullest."

Celebrate Life

For DJ and me, celebrating life has been found in precious little moments. Savor those times, big or small. They could be found on a hike that connects you to nature, or while pausing to view the splendor of a sunset. They could pour forth at a gathering of family—at a wedding in Sedona. Or elsewhere. Those precious moments might also be discovered at a gallery through a piece of art.

The spirit of celebration will take root in your heart when you purposefully seek it out. Take the time to celebrate in quiet gratitude, or with triumphant jubilation, for the many blessings you receive.

Most likely, those remembrances will touch your life forever.

Find Your Circle

My pastor, Adam Hamilton, just recently shared this message in his Sunday sermon: No matter what the adversity is that you experience in your life, don't give up. Persevere.

For DJ and me, the first week after getting the breast cancer diagnosis set the tone for this new unplanned, divergent path we were suddenly taking. From the very beginning, we recognized just how blessed we were to have deeply caring and compassionate friends who surrounded us with love in a sacred circle at the Colorado Chautauqua that cool autumn day in September. Clearly, love reverberated deep inside and made it possible for us to see into each other's souls.

In your own personal circumstances, create a sacred circle when faced with adversity. Your circle may be filled with family and friends who offer their love, concern, kindness, and support. You might find your circle includes only one special person who lifts you up. It's also conceivable that you find guidance or learn from someone else's experience in dealing with a similar challenge. Your circle just might be filled with your faith, and will grasp the divine presence of God wrapped around you.

When you are alone—and you will feel alone and distracted at times—quiet your mind and listen for your inner voice. Be ready to boldly move forward in faith and have the courage to fight on.

Live in the Moment

In those first weeks following my diagnosis, questions surrounded me as I grasped my situation and the uncertainty of what was awaiting me. What was my destiny? I felt as if my life were suddenly out of control. I couldn't express what was raging inside of me.

Then, I looked to God and surrendered to Him. He turned my weakness and helplessness into strength. I still had moments of darkness and pain, yet I knew deep in my soul that He was with me, and He placed others in my life to lean on. And boy, did I need those relationships to help lift me up.

Meditate on the healing deep within you. Breathe in the acts of kindness. Find comfort in the challenging times. Live joyfully. Focus on the present. Live in the moment.

Embrace an Attitude of Gratitude

DJ recently said, "Even in our deepest darkest valleys, we find ways to celebrate life."

That's so true. His thought ties back to something our friend Deena once shared, "It's all about having an attitude of gratitude."

Everyone faces storms in their life. A serious illness, a broken heart, the loss of a loved one, or some other adversity in one's labyrinth of life. When those times occur, be open to embracing head-on what may be a life-changing moment. Those dark periods may just open your heart and soul to new ways of thinking, creating, doing, and living. By changing your mindset

from one of anger, sadness, and/or fear to an attitude of gratitude, you will reap abundant blessings.
I learned when you shift your day-to-day focus to the
blessings and world that surround you, you will get
through the difficult times. Embrace those times with
an attitude of gratitude!

Believing Is Seeing

Conventional thinking tells us that we must see
something to believe in it. Over the years, I've
challenged this myopic reasoning. I've come to
understand that if you truly believe, you will see. God
gives us a way to do what we couldn't do on our own
if we believe. He gives us the strength and dares us to
move forward in faith, love, and hope in co-creating
a vision and turning it into reality. The Bible verse 2
Corinthians 5:7 proclaims, "We live by faith, not by
sight."

No matter how great the challenge in our lives,
trust that God will help you make it through. This
wisdom can help you through difficulties in your
life or to have the confidence to see a visionary plan
through to its completion. Believe it, then you will see
it.

Tune In

Tune in to what's going on in the world around you.
In my previous book, *Come Together, Think Ahead*,
I describe the concept of coincidence, which has
also been called synchronicity. You may experience
unexpected incidents in your life. Happenings you

never could have imagined. I find these times tend to show up out of nowhere, but these occurrences respond to our intentions.

Joseph Jaworski, in his book, *Synchronicity: The Inner Path of Leadership,* describes it as a natural unfolding in which an event that could have never been predicted seems to guide us along our journey.

My life coach, Lee Kaiser, described synchronicity as a "vibrational relationship." He taught that "people … seemingly appear from nowhere to respond, and connect with, our intentions. It is a flood of connections that allows highly intentional people to create in big ways."

I believe these connections are not just a fluke or an accident. They are a phenomenon, a wonder, or perhaps even a miracle.

Einstein has an interesting way of defining this concept. His view of coincidence "is God's way of remaining anonymous." I like this description the best. Because I believe God is ever present in our lives as He and His angels quietly watch over and guide us.

Be open and TUNE IN.

Let Your Voice Be Heard

The train station story made me realize that many of us have faced times in life when it seems every door is closed. As a result, we might just want to fade into the background. If we idly sit back and stay silent, we can become frustrated and confused. The question is: How will you confront life's obstacles and challenges head on?

Don't be afraid to speak up. Ask questions. Listen

to your inner voice. Stay confident. And express yourself. Wherever life takes you—going through a divorce, confronting a serious illness, being abused or bullied, dealing with a work-related issue, or being left behind at the train station—let your voice be heard.

Expect the Unexpected

Tap into the world that surrounds you. Always be prepared for the possibility that those unexpected blessings in life have been chosen for you. These blessings are all there waiting to happen through you. You'll experience a depth of love, joy, peace, and fulfillment that you've never imagined. And sometimes, you may experience challenging times that turn out to be some of the greatest blessings of all.

And remember this: Never leave home without your glasses.

Keep Hope Alive

The morning after hearing the dreadful news about Hayden, I went up to my writing space in the loft to pack my computer and other papers as we were preparing to head home to Kansas City. While opening my desk drawer to search for a pen and notepad, an unfamiliar pink memo sheet laid face up and had the words *Keep Hope Alive* printed on it in my handwriting. Below these three words I had referenced two scriptures, John 3:16 and Ezekiel 37:5.

John 3:16 is likely the most quoted Bible verse of all and one of my favorites since childhood. The verse,

"For God so loved the world, He gave His one and only son, that whoever believes in Him, shall have eternal life," was spoken by Jesus to Nicodemus about being born again. He was emphasizing the transformation of a person's earthly life into a heavenly everlasting life. The freed butterfly symbolizes this transformation of a new creation and resurrection.

In the other scripture, Ezekiel 37:5 prophesizes about dry bones (death) and new life. "This is what the Sovereign Lord says to these bones: I will make breath enter you, and you will come to life." I believe the Lord has placed new breath in Hayden, and his soul has been resurrected in heaven.

Losing a child is unimaginable, but God works in mysterious ways to help us find the courage to face our darkest moments and discover splendor from this wounded space. God's love never departs from us. I also know Hayden's love will forever surround me.

In those moments of acknowledging the deeper meanings of Hayden's "Just Breathe" painting and seeing the black and blue butterfly, it encouraged me to keep my hope alive. Both the wooden sign and the butterfly spoke of transformation, renewal, and resurrection for eternal life as promised by God through His son, Jesus. In fact, I take refuge not only believing it to be so, but also counting on it.

Profess Your Intentions

There are a number of signs in our home. They are pieces of art with words of inspiration and wisdom. They remind us of important truths.

Jordan gave me one of those pieces of art as a

birthday gift recently. It is a framed window, about twenty-four inches wide and thirty inches tall, and it hangs above my writing desk in the loft at our lake cabin. The piece depicts a contemporary design of an oak tree with deep roots. One side of the tree is full of leaves, and on the other side the leaves are fluttering away and transforming into what appears to be birds and butterflies. These prophetic words are painted in white lettering on glass:

WINGS
to show you what
you can become

ROOTS
to remind you
where you're from

On my own path of discovery, I've found my life to be deeply rooted in transformational experiences that have been beautiful, joyful, and, at times, shattering. All these soulful encounters have led to what I am choosing to become.

Life is filled with abundance should we choose to see it that way. When your days seem darkest and chaotic, have the courage and confidence to set your intentions and begin to rescript your life by imagining what's possible. Change your mindset and embrace the possibilities showing up through you. With God's grace, seek the life that is waiting for you.

There is another sign in our lake cabin. It is on the porch, a reminder to us as we leave home and enter the world each day. It reads:

IF YOU THINK SUNSHINE BRINGS HAPPINESS,

THEN YOU HAVEN'T DANCED IN THE RAIN.

In Memoriam
Dr. Leland "Lee" Kaiser
(1936– 2019)

LEE KAISER PASSED AWAY on January 4, 2019. He was filled with wisdom, kindness, optimism, and a strong faith, and, as a mentor, he had a profound impact on my life. In his teachings, Lee taught that "to create a preferred future, and to step in to who we will become, requires that we imagine what this could look like." He professed that you create your script by starting with "becoming" questions.

I learned from Lee that by setting your intentions in the present tense, you state your desire of your future self. Imagine yourself already there for what may have been unimaginable before. Consciously write a script "that gives you a sense of purpose and meaning, personal and spiritual growth, and your life as a journey." What's your next chapter of "becoming"? Choose more consciously.

It was Lee's hope to make a positive and meaningful change in the world, and, by sharing his insights, he did just that. Here are a few of his "wisdomisms":

"Changing your mind changes your future."

"We create boundaries when we want to avoid responsibility."

"The future is determined by what we do."

"We cannot have what we cannot imagine."

"If you hold the intention, you've given God permission to intervene."

"Every story has an end,
but in life every end
is a new beginning ..."

Acknowledgments

GARY MARX, MY EDITOR and friend, played a major part in collaborating with me on this book. He far exceeded my expectations. His advice, notes, and encouragement added much value in helping to guide the direction of Daring to Dance Again. What a blessing it's been to work with him.

I'm also grateful for the team of dedicated professionals from Mission Point Press—the project's leader, Doug Weaver, business manager and partner; Rebecca Prather, copy editor; Ruth Campbell, the project's proofreader; Sarah Meiers, Tricia Frey, and Hart Cauchy of the marketing group; and website designer Noah Shaw.

Thanks to all of you.

I also want to acknowledge two very special people in my life ... truly angels in my life: my husband DJ and daughter Jordan, who have been on this journey with me from Day One. Their support, encouragement, and insight have been a major influence in this collaboration. Quite simply, their love, support, and belief in me made all the difference in completing this memoir.

About the Author

JUDITH K. SABBERT (JUDY) grew up on a farm outside of White Cloud, Kansas, a community of 300 people at the time. She went on to complete three degrees: a bachelor's and a master's in Applied Behavioral Science from the University of Kansas and a second master's in Administration from Central Michigan University. She served as president of the nationally recognized and award-winning Heartland Foundation (aka Mosaic Life Care Foundation), ending a 30-year career with the nonprofit in 2018.

In 2015, Judith released her first book, *Come Together, Think Ahead,* that focused on a collective leadership approach to transform communities and people's lives. Her work recognized that "Each of us is progress, each of us is potential, each of us is possibility, but only if we THINK AHEAD." Healthy Communities and emPowerU were two of the innovative programs she co-created and led at the foundation. In 2019, the organization established the Judith K. Sabbert Spark Award, an annual recognition presented to young people who are civically engaged and take on community projects that have had an impact on other people's lives.

Instead of retirement, Judy chose "re-firement." If she's not in her loft writing, she is seeking new life adventures with her husband, DJ. Together they have four children and five grandchildren.

Contact the author at www.JudithSabbert.com.

Bibliography

Artwork

Just Breathe, Hayden Muck
Sedona at Dusk, Jan Sitts
The Angel, Robin John Anderson
The Bird, Josh Hamilton
The Pearls of Wisdom, Teresa Pilliccio
Wings and Roots, Beth Ostmann

Books

Coelho, Paulo. *The Alchemist.* New York: HarperTorch, 2006.

Jacobs, Hollye. *The Silver Lining: A Supportive and Insightful Guide to Breast Cancer.* Dallas, TX: Brown Books Publishing, 2014.

Jakes, T. D. *The Lady, Her Lover, and Her Lord.* New York: Berkley Books, published by The Berkley Publishing Group, a division of Penguin Putnam Inc., 1998.

Jaworski, Joseph. *Synchronicity: The Inner Path of Leadership*. San Francisco: Berrett-Koehler Publishers Inc., 1996.

Jung, Carl Gustav. *Synchronicity: An Acausal Connecting Principle*. England: Routledge, 1985.

Kneece, Judy K. *Breast Cancer Treatment Handbook, 9th Edition*. North Charleston, South Carolina: EduCare Publishing Inc., 2017.

Lucado, Max. *Grace for Each Moment*. Bloomingdale, IL: Christian Art Gifts, 2011 (Second Edition).

Olson, Bob. *Answers About the Afterlife: A Private Investigator's 15-year Research Unlocks the Mysteries of Life after Death*. Kennebunkport, ME: Building Bridges Press, 2014.

Sabbert, Bertha. *A Few of My Favorite Things: From the FILE of Bertha Sabbert*. Self-published.

Sabbert, Judith K. *Come Together, Think Ahead*. Traverse City, MI; Kansas City, MO: Chandler Lake Books, 2015.

Sillers, Tia, and Mark D. Sanders. *I Hope You Dance*. Nashville, TN: Rutledge Hill Press, 2000.

Wilkinson, Bruce H. *The Prayer of Jabez: Breaking Through to the Blessed Life*. Sisters, OR: Multnomah Publishers Inc., 2000.

Women of Destiny Bible. (New King James Version). Nashville: Thomas Nelson, 1999.

Young, Sarah. *Jesus is Calling: Enjoying Peace in His Presence*. Nashville, Dallas, Mexico City, Rio De Janeiro: Thomas Nelson, 2004, 2011.

Devotionals and Poems

Earekson Tada, Joni. "Shattered Glass." NIV Women's Devotional Bible 2. Grand Rapids, MI: The Zondervan Corporation, 1990.

Hale, Edward Everett. *I May Only Be One, But I Am Still One.* https://www.epistle.us/poetry/iamonlyone.html.

Mahoe, Sharon. "Gravity at Work." NIV Women's Devotional Bible 2. Grand Rapids, MI: The Zondervan Corporation, 1990.

Websites

American Society of Plastic Surgeons. https://www.ASPS.org.

Einstein, Albert. "Coincidence is God's Way of Remaining Anonymous." Good Reads. http://goodreads.com/quotes.

"Conditions of Colon Cancer." Facty Health. http://www.factyhealth.com/conditions/cancer.

"Breast Cancer Statistics." National Breast Cancer Foundation. http://www.nationalbreastcancer.org.

"Colon Cancer". WebMD. http://www.webmd.org/coloncancer.